Soviet Economic Assistance
to the
Less Developed Countries

Soviet Economic Assistance
to the
Less Developed Countries

A Statistical Analysis

QUINTIN V. S. BACH

CLARENDON PRESS · OXFORD
1987

Oxford University Press, Walton Street, Oxford OX2 6DP

Oxford New York Toronto
Delhi Bombay Calcutta Madras Karachi
Kuala Lumpur Singapore Hong Kong Tokyo
Nairobi Dar es Salaam Cape Town
Melbourne Auckland

and associated companies in
Beirut Berlin Ibadan Nicosia

Oxford is a trade mark of Oxford University Press

Published in the United States
by Oxford University Press, New York

British Library Cataloguing in Publication Data
Bach, Quintin
Soviet economic assistance to the less
developed countries: a statistical analysis.
1. Economic assistance, Russian—Statistics
I. Title
338.91′47′01724021   HC60
ISBN 0-19-828572-8

Library of Congress Cataloging in Publication Data
Bach, Quintin.
Soviet economic assistance to the less developed
countries.
Bibliography: p.
Includes index.
1. Economic Assistance, Russian—Developing
countries—Statistics. I. Title.
HC60.B23   1987   338.91′47′01724   87-20349
ISBN 0-19-828572-8

Typeset by Joshua Associates Ltd, Oxford
Printed and bound in Great Britain by
Biddles Ltd, Guildford and King's Lynn

PREFACE

These tables represent an attempt to compile a complete and unbiased set of statistics on Soviet economic development assistance to the less developed countries (LDCs) since it started generally in 1954. Such a compendium has never previously been published in the USSR or outside because, although a value has normally been attached to agreements, disbursements have only been made in the form of goods and services rather than finance, and valuation of this assistance is not therefore simply a matter of financial arithmetic.

The CIA were the first to publish general statistics of Soviet economic aid for the years 1977 to 1979, with cumulative figures going back to 1954. They have not published every year since, however; no rationale was given for the estimates; they show some internal inconsistencies; and they do not include Soviet assistance to the LDC members of the Council for Mutual Economic Assistance (CMEA, often referred to as Comecon), nor Laos, Cambodia, or North Korea. The Development Assistance Directorate of OECD has been publishing some statistics on this subject since then in 'Development Cooperation', the Chairman's annual report, and did include Cuba, North Korea, and Vietnam—but not Mongolia until 1984, nor do they produce statistics for individual recipient countries nor make estimates before 1970. The British Foreign and Commonwealth Office published Foreign Policy Documents covering Soviet aid in the years 1970–78, 1976–82, and 1976–83; but they also do not go back before 1970, they include Mongolia only after 1976, and—like OECD—do not make estimates for individual countries, while repayments are only suggested by their listing of some 'net' figures.

Soviet spokesmen in UN bodies have given global Soviet aid figures for the years 1976–80 and for individual years since, but have given no breakdown by recipient country or type of aid. The Soviet annual *Vneshnyaya Torgovlya SSSRa* statistical handbook gives deliveries under economic and technical agreements from 1955 to 1970 and from 1972 to the present, but it leaves out many countries which have certainly received Soviet asssistance on 'aid' terms, such as Guinea Bissau, Madagascar, and Mozambique. Some deliveries, such as those to Nigeria in the 1980s, are not on 'aid' terms, and by definition such deliveries could not include technical assistance which is certainly acceptable as 'aid'.

No attempt is made in these tables to include all forms of assistance that the Soviet Union has given to the LDCs. The objective is limited to showing as accurately as the evidence permits the level of Soviet economic development aid to the individual LDCs. This excludes all types of military assistance except where the construction of an airfield or a port for economic development purposes could have a military implication; for the rest military assistance is not normally published, and even when a figure is available the terms may not be, so that it would be difficult to separate 'aid' from commercial transactions—besides only marginally, perhaps, affecting economic development. Price subsidies are excluded on the basis of the UN and OECD criterion that such subsidies are only admissible as 'aid' if they are not bilateral and therefore fully competitive. OECD statistics accept scholarships at UN valuations, but have not been included here as not strictly economic development aid; besides which it is difficult to attach to them a proper value since they are almost exclusively payable in domestic roubles. The Soviet spokesmen, in giving global Soviet aid statistics, included such immeasurables as 'subsidies on technical know-how', 'assistance on transport', and 'aid in fisheries' which normally means the right to fish in the LDC's local waters in exchange for some assistance to its fisheries industry or a proportion of the fish catch; these categories have also been excluded.

With less justification, perhaps, I have excluded Soviet gifts of equipment for hospitals, educational establishments, and sports and municipal buildings unless contained in normal economic agreements since it is otherwise difficult to give them a fair valuation; in any case the total would not greatly affect the over-all figures.

In their agreements with the LDCs the Russians give a general value to a project, and apparently in the contracts give a particular valuation to a major sector—a blast furnace, a rolling mill, or a distillation column—for the purpose of showing the start of interest payments or repayments. Deliveries of both the whole and individual parts are often spread over two or more years, and no exact figure can be produced for individual years—even if all years were co-terminous (most countries use financial years for their statistics). The closest one can therefore get to an accurate assessment is the method used here: to monitor progress in the construction of such projects, to apportion exenditure for technical assistance, and to be guided by trade statistics or statistics of Soviet deliveries under economic and technical co-operation agreements in order to arrive at a year-by-year estimate of disbursement as a proportion of the value of the original agreement. If I have erred to any extent in my compilation of these figures, it is likely to have been in the direction of assuming that projects were completed by a certain date which were in practice completed later or even not constructed at all. The result is that disbursement figures may be a little high, and therefore also the repayment and interest statistics which are calculated from the disbursement figures.

In an effort to reduce such errors and to test the methods and provisional results, I have been very fortunate in being able to discuss them with officials of the World Bank and the IMF in Washington, and of a representative cross-section of thirteen of the recipient LDCs involved. An added bonus was that I was able to discuss them with the Soviet representatives for economic co-operation in eight of these countries. From all these people I have had nothing but help and encouragement, and they will receive individual acknowledgement elsewhere. They were all, however, taken somewhat by surprise by my approach to this question, and while they are certainly to be thanked for correcting many errors, I alone can be held responsible for those that persist.

I am extremely grateful to the London School of Economics and Political Science for admitting me as a visitor and allowing me to benefit from the library and many other facilities, by no means least the unstinting help of their administrative staff; to Dr Michael Leifer and the members of the Steering Committee of the LSE Centre for International Studies, and latterly to Professor Fred Halliday of the International Relations Department for having offered me a home and the benefit of their collective wisdom; to the Economic and Social Research Council for making my research and the contributory travel possible; and to the Nuffield Foundation for having given invaluable assistance in a particular aspect of the research. My brother Ashley spent many months painstakingly putting the statistics on to a computer, thereby stirring up a hornet's nest of arithmetical and other inaccuracies and easing the task, for me at least, of amendment and revision. My final acknowledgement is to Professor Peter Wiles, whose touching faith and inimitable support give him a burdensome share of responsibility for this creation.

Q.V.S.B.
January 1987

CONTENTS

SEMANTICS

SOVIET ECONOMIC CO-OPERATION

In referring to their economic relations with the less developed countries (LDCs), the Soviet official Collection of Treaties used the word 'pomoshch' (aid or assistance) in a few cases in the late 1950s, usually only where grants for hospitals, schools, etc. were concerned. In one case, however, it was used in a normal agreement with twelve years' repayment and $2\frac{1}{2}\%$ interest—the first Aswan Dam agreement with Egypt.

Apart from these exceptions, Soviet sources do not use the word for aid in referring to their economic relations with the LDCs. The Soviet Union contends that economic aid is compensation paid by the former colonialist powers for past exploitation and that, never having been a colonialist power itself, it owes no such compensation. Soviet economic relations with the LDCs are presumed to be mutually beneficial, and therefore those economic agreements which include Soviet credits on concessional terms are called 'co-operation' agreements. Such agreements may, however, have repayment and interest terms which fall below the level of 25% grant element* accepted by the UN and OECD as the minimum concessionality to be included in the 'aid' category. For the purposes of these tables the 25% barrier has been applied, and therefore not all Soviet co-operation agreements have been included. To differentiate between Soviet agreements that are above and below the 25% limit, I have had to use the word 'aid' to apply to those agreements and terms which are above that limit.

RUSSIANS

An infuriating *lacuna* in the English language is the absence of a single word which refers to all the Soviet people, since 'Soviets' are after all only councils. With all due apologies, therefore, to the great and growing number of Soviet citizens who are not Great Russians—including Mr V. Kilva in Tanzania and Eng. Askold Dralo in Cairo, both very helpful members of the Soviet economic teams—I have to admit to having been occasionally forced to use the word 'Russians' to encompass all the Soviet nationalities.

* A measure of the concessionality of the credit based on its life, grace period, interest rate, and frequency of repayments—see pp. xvi–xvii below.

A HISTORICAL NOTE

From 1917 to the death of Stalin the Soviet Union had very little economic contact with what are now called the less developed countries (LDC's). For much of the period many were under colonial rule, and most of the others were closely linked with the USA. Before the Second World War direct Soviet trade with these countries was negligible, and even by the early 1950s it had reached only about 4% of total Soviet trade, with the balance heavily against the USSR. Before 1954 only three countries had signed economic co-operation agreements with the Soviet Union on 'aid' terms.* Mongolia was said** to have had credit valued in total at $225m, presumably all on aid terms, by 1956; of this most had probably been spent and a lot repaid by that time. Turkey was given an $8m credit in 1934 for the construction of textile mills, also on aid terms. In 1949 North Korea received a Soviet trade credit which may have been on aid terms, but the fact that all debts under this credit were written off by the Soviet Union in 1953 certainly brought it into that category; at the same time North Korea was awarded a new credit on generous terms for rehabilitation and development in the aftermath of the Korean War. The Turkish 1934 credit and the early North Korean credit are excluded from the tables as not impinging on the period covered, but the Mongolian credits and the 1953 North Korean credit are included since they cannot be totally separated from this period.

In 1954 and 1955 Soviet economic co-operation was put on a more formal footing. In 1954 two agreements were signed with Afghanistan which set the general pattern for such agreements, and in 1955 a massive $136m credit was opened with India for the construction of Bhilai iron and steel works on terms which were to become more or less standard for twenty years—repayments in twelve annual instalments starting a year after the delivery of the materials and equipment, or the provision of the technical assistance, either for the complete project or, as in this case, for a major sector such as a blast furnace or a rolling mill, with interest at $2\frac{1}{2}$% payable from 1 January following delivery. In most cases also, as in the Bhilai agreement, the recipient country has the option to repay in goods rather than in convertible currency.

In 1955 Soviet economic co-operation was further formalized by the setting up of a State body to run it, the *Gosudarstvennoye upravleniye po*

---

* i.e. better than 25% grant element—see pp. xvi–xvii below.
** Marshall I. Goldman, *Soviet Foreign Aid*, Praeger 1967, p. 37.

delam ekonomicheskikh svyazey so stranami narodnoy demokratii (GUES), the State Directorate for matters concerned with the Economic Links with Countries of National Democracy. It was up-graded to a State Committee in 1957, and its title changed to the *Gosudarstvennyy komitet Soveta Ministrov SSSR po vneshnim ekonomicheskim svyazyam* (GKES), the State Committee of the USSR Council of Ministers for Foreign Economic Links. Its first Chairman, with ministerial rank, was M. G. Pervukhin, but he was succeeded after only one year by Semyon Andreyevich Skachkov, who became synonymous with the GKES and remained there for nearly 25 years until the death of Brezhnev.

The function of the GKES has been to administer the resources made available to it by Gosplan. It negotiates the agreements with the individual LDCs, and in those countries where it has permanent representatives it can suggest new projects. It acts as broker between the two governments and the industrial and agricultural organizations of the recipient countries and the Soviet production ministries, monitors progress in the execution of projects, and, in co-operation with the Soviet Ministry of Foreign Trade and the State Bank, overseas repayments and interest payments. In the event of a change of government, such as in India in 1977 or Iran in 1979, the Chairman of the GKES has often been the first senior Soviet official to pay a visit to the new regime in order to smooth the way to an orderly continuation of work on the Soviet-assisted projects. The GKES is not responsible for industrial training, which comes under the aegis of the relevant Soviet production Ministry; nor for the fisheries agreements, which are negotiated directly by the Soviet Ministry for Fisheries; nor for scholarships, which are awarded through the Soviet Ministry of Foreign Affairs and the local Soviet embassies. The GKES does not have representatives in all the LDCs which receive Soviet aid; there have not been any in most of the South American countries, for example, nor in Cameroon, Cape Verde, Jordan, Madagascar, Mozambique, or Sierra Leone. Presumably this depends mainly on the scale of Soviet involvement, but in the case of the South American countries it is probably because these projects are regarded by the Russians as commercial, and it is only coincidental that the terms come into the aid category.

Agreements on co-operation in economic development on aid terms were signed by the USSR with 57 countries between 1954 and 1983. Of these, it is estimated that 29 were still drawing on Soviet credits at the end of 1983. The highest total of new agreements in one year was awarded in 1980, at $5.7 billion in round figures. There were other peaks in 1960/61, 1965/66, 1971, and 1976 coinciding with the start of Five Year Plans both in the USSR and frequently in some of the recipient countries. The peak value of new agreements to non-CMEA countries was also in 1980, with large agreements with Afghanistan, India, Peru, and South Yemen. These agreements, however, showed less of a tendency to follow a lustral pattern than those with CMEA countries.

Disbursement of Soviet economic assistance has risen steadily, with few hiccoughs, from $64m in 1957 to $2.4 billion in 1983—although in constant prices the picture is a little different (see the note and table of Soviet aid in fixed prices and the histograms on pp. 6–9). The slight downturns in 1969/70 and 1980 coincided with the start of new Five Year Plans, when presumably the new projects were not yet properly underway. Aid disbursement to the non-CMEA countries fell from a peak in 1971, partly perhaps attributable to the uncertainties caused by the oil crisis, over the following three or four years, and did not reach that total again until 1979. Much of the increase in 1982 and 1983 is accounted for by a considerable increase in aid of all kinds to Afghanistan, but also to the construction and expansion of steel works in India, the increase in the capacity of the İzmir oil refinery in Turkey, the construction of the Karachi steel works in Pakistan, and generous aid of all kinds to South Yemen.

Repayments and interest payments taken together surpassed new aid to the three CMEA countries in 1971 and 1972, and were only a little less in 1969, 1970, and 1973. Normally, however, such payments have been between one third and one quarter of new drawings. For the non-CMEA countries net transfer was also negative in 1974 to 1978, and after that hovered around two thirds of new aid. Some of the Soviet Union's long-standing customers, such as Egypt, Iran, Iraq, and Turkey (and India until the start of the new steel works in 1982) have had repayments and interest exceeding drawings for some considerable time.

METHODOLOGY AND ASSUMPTIONS

Types of aid. These statistics cover economic development assistance only. They do not include 'humanitarian' assistance such as gifts of emergency food and clothing, or gifts of equipment for hospitals, schools, or sports centres since they are difficult to value and, since bilateral, could not be accepted as 'aid' under OECD criteria; in any case they would not greatly affect the totals. Training costs are included when part of credit agreements, but scholarships have not been counted since they are mainly payable in Soviet domestic roubles which are difficult to value in $US terms and, being negotiated through the Soviet Ministry of Foreign Affairs rather than the GKES, can be excluded from the statistics of economic development—although the OECD does include scholarships as 'aid' both for Western countries and for the Soviet Union. All military aid has also been excluded as not being directly concerned with economic development.

The biggest problem lies in the question of the admissibility of favourable prices as 'aid'. Since 1974 the Soviet Union has offered all CMEA countries Soviet oil at the average world price of the previous five years, thereby providing a considerable subsidy in the second half of the 1970s to Cuba, Mongolia, and Vietnam *inter alios*. The largest Soviet price subsidy, however, is in the price paid for Cuban sugar in comparison with the world price, and for much of the time the Soviet price for Cuban nickel has also been above the world price. Table 1 shows these apparent subsidies to Cuba, with direct economic development assistance added for comparison purposes. The price subsidies have been calculated from the quantities and prices derived from Soviet trade statistics compared to the average annual world price; the project aid figures are taken from the estimates on pages 51–3 below.

Under OECD rules the difference between current world oil prices and the price at which it is sold to the LDC would only be admissible as 'aid' if the donor country had bought the oil for convertible currency and sold it at a lower price with no trade strings attached. As far as sugar and nickel purchases are concerned here, they would also only be admissible as 'aid' if they had been bought at this favourable price in convertible currency, again with no trade strings attached. All these Soviet transactions have, however, been entirely bilateral and are not admissible *de jure* as 'aid'. But is this attitude totally unjustified? I have dealt with this subject in a Note in *Soviet Studies*.* Briefly rehearsing

* *Soviet Studies* (Glasgow), vol. xxxvii, no. 2, April 1985, pp. 269–75.

Table 1   Soviet Price Subsidies and Project Aid to Cuba, 1970–1983
($US millions)

Year	Sugar	Oil	Nickel	Total Price Subsidies	Project Aid	Total
1970	162.0	12.0	35.0	209.0	2	211.0
1971	58.5	32.2	41.0	131.7	3	134.7
1972	−16.5	16.9	15.6	16.0	3	19.0
1973	102.4	31.2	32.7	166.3	3	169.3
1974	−416.1	453.1	16.6	53.6	82	135.6
1975	537.0	307.1	−3.5	840.6	120	960.6
1976	1119.1	371.8	12.0	1502.9	133	1635.9
1977	1646.5	354.2	40.1	2040.8	185	2225.8
1978	2448.8	192.0	12.6	2653.4	300	2953.4
1979	2322.2	489.5	−31.5	2780.2	400	3180.2
1980	1183.2	1372.5	−36.8	2518.9	300	2818.9
1981	1388.1	1526.9	39.5	2954.5	463	3417.5
1982	2623.7	969.0	49.5	3642.2	530	4172.2
1983	3085.0	199.0	50.0	3334.0	530	3864.0
TOTALS	16243.9	6327.4	272.8	22844.1	3054	25898.1

these arguments, the Soviet Professor B. S. Vagranov has shown** that there were four categories of Soviet export prices, the highest being for economic assistance and the lowest for convertible currency, and where comparisons of such prices were possible this seems to be supported by the facts. For instance, if one takes the average Soviet export price in any one year as 100, the Cuban purchase price of a light car was 132, a motorcycle 197, urea 144, cement 121, plywood 115, and window glass 171 (compared with the price of window glass in the same year to the USA of 60). While there may be some net element of price subsidy to Cuba, therefore, it cannot be fully counted and the attitude of OECD in not admitting such subsidies in full under these circumstances seems justified.

Choice of recipient countries. The countries considered are all those which fall into the United Nations category of Less Developed Country, with the exclusion of those on mainland Europe (Romania, Bulgaria, Yugoslavia, Portugal, and Spain—Greece in any case had no economic co-operation with the USSR before 1983); Turkey has been included as being not only mainland Europe. China has been excluded as being in a very different general category. Those countries described as 'CMEA' are, of course, those which belonged at the end of the period regardless of the date they joined.

** *Foreign Trade of the Socialist Countries: Theoretical Problems*, Moscow 1966.

Basic types of economic assistance. There are five basic types of economic development assistance which are included in the present statistics: for a single project; for a series of projects to be built under a framework credit; for a framework credit to be drawn on by the LDCs, mainly the CMEA members, during a fixed period of economic development such as a Five Year Plan; for trade credits for the supply of Soviet goods to be sold in the LDC to generate local currency to help cover local development costs or the expenses of Soviet advisers; and finally for trade credits fixed at a maximum figure for the purchase of Soviet industrial products in an effort to off-set some of the trade imbalance—especially, for instance, with some South American countries. The left-hand margin of the tables gives the title of the agreement as given in the Soviet Treaty series or, if not in that series, it names the project or stated purpose of the credit.

A = Agreements. The first horizontal line of each credit shows the value given to the agreement in the year it was signed. It may have originally been expressed in $US, £ Sterling, French francs, foreign trade roubles, or in the LDCs own currency, but for the sake of consistency and comparison it has always been converted into the current $US value. It can be assumed that such prices are in line with reigning world prices since the LDC would not accept the cost if it were too high, and the Soviet Union claims mutual benefit and would not therefore fix it too low.* Agreements with the CMEA countries are expressed in roubles; these have been taken as foreign trade roubles since the alternative would be a statistical nightmare—but since one of the Soviet agreements with Mongolia specifies 'foreign trade roubles', by implication there at least all other agreements have been made in domestic roubles.

T = Terms. These are in the first column of the tables, and are derived from the text of the agreement or from press or radio reports. By the A is the grant element, measuring in per cent the level of concessionality of the agreement, taking into account the year's grace (or more if agreed), the number of years for repayment (opposite the R—if this reads, for example 3 + 12 the 3 is the grace period), and the interest rate (opposite the I). The grant element is taken from the tables compiled by the Development Assistance Directorate of OECD according to the formula:

---

* For a discussion of the foreign trade and domestic roubles and their relative values and price changes according to different criteria, see *Soviet Studies*, Glasgow, *loc. cit.*

$$GE = 100 \times (1 - \frac{r/a}{d}) \left[\frac{1 - \dfrac{1}{(1+d)^{aG}} - \dfrac{1}{(1+d)^{nM}}}{D(aM - aG)} \right]$$

where GE = grant element as a percentage of concessionality
   r = annual interest on the credit
   a = number of payments per annum
   d = discount rate per period, i.e. $(1.1)^{\frac{1}{n}}$ giving a compound annual rate of 10%
   G = grace period, the interval to the first repayment
   M = maturity, the life of the loan from agreement to final payment

Only agreements with a grant element of 25% or better are considered by the United Nations and OECD to be on 'aid' terms, and this has therefore been used as the cut-off point here.

D = Disbursement. Since Soviet economic assistance is normally distributed in the form of goods and services rather that in monetary form, disbursement can only be measured according to the amount of the original agreement and progress in its execution. *This has been the basic task of the present research*. The Russians have published statistics of what they claim as the total value of all their economic assistance to the LDCs for the period 1976–80 and for individual subsequent years, but this includes various categories of assistance which are not accepted as 'aid' under UN and OECD criteria; and since they give no breakdown by category, amounts, or recipient country they cannot be properly evaluated or analysed.* The Russians have also published in their trade statistics a category of deliveries under economic and technical agreements since 1954. These figures are not very different in many cases from those produced in these tables; but they exclude many countries which have certainly received Soviet assistance (see those asterisked in the list of LDCs which have made 'aid' agreements with the USSR on p. xxii below), by definition they appear to exclude technical assistance, and they have clearly included deliveries (for example to Nigeria in recent years) which are not on 'aid' terms. They also gave no statistics for 1971. A few countries have published their own statistics of drawings under Soviet agreements, but they are often very different from Soviet figures and too few to provide a consistent picture for all countries.

In the case of a single project the present tables base the drawings of Soviet credits on a curve of expenditure; this curve starts before

* See *Soviet Studies loc. cit.*

construction gets under way, with the costs of planning and pre-construction deliveries, rises to a peak just before half-way *ex post facto* through construction, and continues for a short time after completion to allow for start-up and run-in. Since drawings are made in the form of goods and services it can be assumed that 100% has been disbursed with the project's completion. In practice there may frequently be cost overruns, as was reported by the Turkish Consortium to the OECD, but these are apparently normally settled on a direct commercial basis unless the subject of a separate agreement.

If an agreement covers several projects, evidence is sought of the construction of each, and if it is clear that some did not get off the ground an effort is made to find out whether the credits were used for other purposes: the Soviet advisers in Cairo told me that those not used by the Egyptians for the specified projects under the 1958 agreement were re-allocated to other projects, whereas in Kenya and Tanzania I learnt that their respective credits of 1964 and 1966 were not used at all.

When a credit is designated for economic development to be drawn at the discretion of the LDC (for example, the 1976 and 1981 credits to Cuba) it is assumed to have been fully taken up if Soviet exports allow for it; in the case of the 1958 and 1960 trade credits to Argentina they clearly did not. Credits for Soviet exports to cover local costs are assumed to have been taken up, as they normally appear to be, within a very short space of time.

R = Repayments. These are calculated according to the terms of the agreement. These specify the interval to first payment, usually twelve months after delivery or after completion of construction of the whole or of a major part of a project. In the tables, unless a grace period over twelve months has been agreed, repayment is assumed to start the year after completion of the project regardless of its complexity unless there is more than one credit (as the two credits for Egypt's Aswan High Dam); if there are more, and when a credit is drawn on over a long period over a considerable range of projects, such as the $333m credit to India in 1966, some staggering of the repayments has been introduced.

The normal method of repayment has been for the debtor country to deposit with the Soviet Bank the amount due in $US, which is repaid to the LDC as the agreed goods are exported to the Soviet Union. Without access to these accounts it is not possible to separate repayments from ordinary trade; but there have been few cases of rescheduling, which have normally been published in a separate agreement; and for simplicity, and to avoid any inadvertent unfairness in suggesting default, repayments have not been amended even in these cases, and the figures are therefore purely theoretical. Exact figures would not in any case affect the overall picture to any great extent.

Interest. This has also been calculated from the terms of the original agreement. Payment starts from the date of delivery, except in the one or two instances (the 1981 $31m credit to Ethiopia, for example) where interest does not start until the end of the grace period. A Turkish official informed me that interest payments were aggregated at the outset and divided into equal payments according to the number of years it is payable (that is, the years for repayment plus any grace period in most instances). This has therefore been assumed in the tables to be the usual practice. The total amount of interest to be paid has therefore been calculated according to the simple formula:

$$I = \frac{0.54\,Crn}{100}$$

where I = total interest payable, C = capital value of the agreement, r = rate of interest in per cent, and n = number of years over which interest is due. Amounts for individual years may be rounded, but are adjusted to give a total as close as possible to the correct figure. Interest payments have not been adjusted for rescheduling and are therefore, like those for repayments, theoretical.

LO = Loan Outstanding after taking into account the original credit and disbursement to date. This has been introduced at the suggestion of several individuals in order to give a running picture of the totals drawn at any time against the total original credits. Also, when taken cumulatively it shows on average how long it takes for Soviet credits to be disbursed: for example, in the grand totals for all countries cumulative agreements in 1969 were just over $9 billion, a figure which was passed by deliveries in 1975, suggesting an average between agreement and disbursement of Soviet aid of around four or five years. When the residue of a credit is transferred to another agreement, such as the 1958 and 1960 credits to Argentina and the 1959 credit to Ethiopia, the 'loan outstanding' is discontinued and it is not in the text.

Soviet Trade Statistics. The annual Soviet publication *Foreign Trade of the USSR: A Statistical Compilation* has contained, from the 1973 edition which also included 1972, a special sub-heading to cover economic co-operation deliveries: it appears in the summary sections at the beginning under the main heading 'Geographical Distribution of Exports of Certain Goods of the USSR by Country'; under '10–19: Machinery, Equipment, and Means of Transport' there is a sub-heading

'Of which Equipment *and Materials* Delivered for Projects under Construction Abroad with the Technical Co-operation of the USSR'. A similar item appeared from 1955 until 1970 under each individual country as item '16: Equipment *and Materials* of Complex Under-takings' (the italics in both cases are mine). The Soviet Union's East European allies and Finland and Yugoslavia are listed as well as those included here. For 1971, between the two presentations, no statistics of this kind were published.

As can be seen from the list of countries which have made economic agreements with the USSR (p. xxii), nineteen of them—those asterisked—were never included in the Soviet lists. These lists also clearly include deliveries under terms which may be below the 25% grant element cut-off: the table for Nigeria, for example, shows deliveries according to the Soviet trade statistics reaching over $300m in 1982 and 1983 which are apparently for the Ajakuta steelworks, but according to the 1976 agreement no credits were involved and the price of the equipment and material would be 'no less favourable than world prices', which can hardly be accepted as concessional. But such Soviet statistics also apparently underestimate the value of Soviet assistance since *a priori* they seem to exclude technical assistance, normally included in co-operation agreements and amounting perhaps to 40% of the total value of the project; it is only in rare cases (see, for example, paragraph 3 of the note on Afghanistan and paragraphs 2 and 3 of the note on Ethiopia) that tangible deliveries are made to cover some of these technical costs.

Prices. The statistics have all been expressed in $US for recognition purposes, but in the main country tables they are in a hybrid form: the agreements are in current $US of the time of the agreement, but in order to show the proportion of an agreement disbursed and repaid at any time these statistics are given in fixed prices of the year of the agreement.

Up to 1971 the $US had a fixed value in relation to the foreign trade rouble, but after that year this rouble has held its theoretical gold content and has therefore had its value constantly adjusted in relation to the $US; this rouble is therefore representative of world prices. To show Soviet aid disbursement in *current prices* it is necessary to convert all drawings after 1971 on the basis of the fluctuations in the $US value, and this has been carried out to produce current price totals by convert-ing the disbursement figures after 1971 for each agreement according to the base year of the agreement's signature. Table 2 has been used as the base.

Repayments and interest payments, as noted above, are apparently given in fixed prices based on the $US value at the time of the agree-ment. The mechanics of repayment and interest payments, however, were based on the $US current value each year rather than on world

Table 2   US$ per Foreign Trade Rouble

Up to 1960	0.25	1977	1.36
Up to 1971	1.11	1978	1.47
1972	1.21	1979	1.53
1973	1.34	1980	1.54
1974	1.32	1981	1.39
1975	1.38	1982	1.38
1976	1.35	1983	1.38

Source: Bank of England, from average daily *Financial Times* rate.

prices, and a joint commission of the two countries met each year to plan the goods to be provided by the LDC for the $US to be paid (which was therefore in current $US prices). Since the Soviet Union and the East European countries complained of losing out on repayments because of the declining $US in the 1970s the system of repayment was generally changed in the early 1980s, and is now based on a basket of currencies.

The current price totals have been converted into *constant 1967 prices* according to Table 3; it gives the average between producer and consumer prices since, although most Soviet aid deliveries were in the producer sector, their deliveries to generate local currency were not, and goods used for repayment would have been very mixed.

Table 3   Purchasing Power of the $US

1954	1.207	1969	0.925
1955	1.209	1970	0.994
1956	1.184	1971	0.852
1957	1.142	1972	0.826
1958	1.114	1973	0.767
1959	1.110	1974	0.678
1960	1.097	1975	0.617
1961	1.092	1976	0.587
1962	1.084	1977	0.551
1963	1.097	1978	0.511
1964	1.070	1979	0.460
1965	1.052	1980	0.406
1966	1.201	1981	0.369
1967	1.000	1982	0.351
1968	0.966	1983	0.345

Source: US Bureau of Labor Statistics.

CHRONOLOGY

OF SIGNATURE OF FIRST
ECONOMIC CO-OPERATION
AGREEMENT WITH THE USSR
BY COUNTRY

Pre-1954	Mongolia (?), Turkey (1934), North Korea (1953)
1954	Afghanistan
1955	India
1956	Indonesia, Yemen Arab Republic
1957	Burma
1958	Argentina*, Egypt, Sri Lanka
1959	Ethiopia, Guinea, Iraq, Nepal
1960	Cuba, Ghana, Vietnam
1961	Mali, Nigeria, Pakistan, Somalia, Sudan, Tunisia
1962	Laos, Turkey (first post-war)
1963	Algeria, Cameroon*, Iran, Kampuchea
1964	Congo (Brazzaville), Kenya*, Syria, Uganda
1965	Senegal
1966	Morocco, Tanzania
1967	Chile, Sierra Leone*, Zambia
1968	Chad
1969	Jordan*, Yemen Peoples' Democratic Republic
1970	Bolivia*, Central Aftrican Republic*, Peru*
1971	Costa Rica*
1972	Bangladesh
1973	—
1974	—
1975	—
1976	Angola, Benin*, Guinea (Bissau)*, Mozambique*
1977	Madagascar*
1978	—
1979	Cape Verde Islands*
1980	—
1981	Nicaragua*
1982	Colombia*, Grenada*, Sao Tomé e Principé*
1983	—

* These countries never appeared in the lists of those receiving deliveries under co-operation agreements in the Soviet trade statistics up to the end of 1983.

TABLES

In all the following tables of agreements, terms, deliveries, interest, and loans outstanding the figures are given in US$m.

GRAND TOTALS

This table gives the sum of the statistics reported, estimated, and calculated by individual country and agreement. The CMEA recipients are, of course, those which were members at the end of 1983.

These totals can be used to compare disbursements, repayments, and interest in relation to the original agreements. For example, it shows that repayments exceeded new disbursements for CMEA recipients in 1971 and 1972, and for non-CMEA recipients in 1974, 1975, and 1976.

The cumulative totals have been included to illustrate the proportion of Soviet economic contracted assistance which has been delivered at any one time; it can also be used to calculate the average period between agreement on a credit and its disbursement (see page xix).

Note D: Includes previous years.

	55	56	57	58	59	60	61	62	63	64	65	66	67	68	69	70	71	72	73	74	75	76	77	78	79	80	81	82	83	55–83
T O T A L S CMEA Countries																														
A			61			200	500	150	16	41	872	243	33	232	188	644		11	380	79	68	3199	111	153	254	3653	2575	284	220	13767
D	2250	2150	9	23	23	21	67	150	165	146	212	243	270	232	158	114	124	133	166	327	352	354	598	805	1036	969	1189	1529	1466	11096
R	145	145	10	10	10	10	10	14	20	20	17	59.3	62.6	68.6	87.3	91.5	126.7	135.9	140.4	140.5	141.7	183.7	185	176.3	174.8	173.8	221.8	218.6	218.5	2873
I	24	24	2.1	2.2	2.3	2.5	2.7	3.7	4.7	7	9.9	11.4	14.2	15.1	17.6	18.4	18.9	19.1	21.1	23.4	24.6	26.3	27.5	28.3	29.9	34	35.8	50.3	77.2	554.2
LO		10	10	62	39	16	195	628	478	329	224	884	641	404	172	202	732	608	486	700	452	168	3013	2526	1874	1092	3776	5162	3917	2671
T O T A L S non-CMEA Countries																														
A	220	215	221	305	423	810	703	190	474	671	262	1021	163	552	425.5	76.7	918	766.3	300.7	360	812.6	864.3	412	172.9	1265	2090	627	716.9	415	16453
D	2030	32	55	63	108	154	190	264	383	416	401	406	458	462	461.1	453.3	475.9	456	429.5	299.9	376.4	375.9	431.1	443.4	668.6	722.4	717	948.7	935.6	11791
R		0.2	0.2	0.2	1.1	3.1	13.6	20.1	25.1	62.8	115	139	156	193	218	247.7	272.7	316.7	340.5	382	419.1	405.7	395.7	402.7	416.9	430.5	452.6	457.2	496.2	6396
I		0.2	0.7	1.1	1.1	3.1	5.5	7.9	13.8	20.4	23.6	30.8	35.9	40.7	45.9	49.1	52.4	60.2	64.8	72	74.2	69.3	66.4	68.7	74.5	82.6	87.4	92.2	96.8	1241
LO	189	372	372	538	780	1095	1751	2264	2018	2109	2364	2224	2839	2544	2634	2598	2222	2664	2974	2845	2906	3342	3830	3811	3541	4137	5504	5414	5182	4662
T O T A L S All Countries																														
A	220	215	282	305	423	1010	1203	340	490	712	1134	1264	196	784	613.5	720.7	918	777.3	680.7	439	880.6	4063	523	325.9	1519	5743	3202	1001	635	30220
D	4280	2182	64	86	131	175	257	414	548	562	613	649	728	694	619.1	567.3	599.9	589	595.5	626.9	728.4	729.9	1029	1248	1705	1691	1906	2478	2402	22887
R	145	145.2	10.2	10.2	11.1	13.1	23.6	34.1	45.1	82.8	132	198.3	218.6	261.6	305.3	339.2	399.4	452.6	480.9	522.5	560.8	589.4	580.7	579	591.7	604.3	674.4	675.8	714.7	9269
I	24	24.2	2.8	3.3	3.4	5.6	8.2	11.6	18.5	27.4	33.5	42.2	50.1	55.8	63.5	67.5	71.3	79.3	85.9	95.4	98.8	95.6	93.9	97	104.4	116.6	123.2	142.5	174	1795
LO	189	382	382	600	819	1111	1946	2892	2496	2438	2588	3108	3480	2948	2806	2800	2954	3272	3460	3545	3358	3510	6843	6337	5415	5229	9280	10576	9099	7333
T O T A L S Cumulative CMEA																														
A	392	607	828	1133	1556	2366	3069	3088	3562	4233	4494	5515	5678	6230	6656	6733	7651	8417	8718	9078	9890	10755	11167	11339	12604	14694	15321	16038	16453	
D	203	235	290	353	461	615	805	1070	1453	1869	2270	2676	3134	3596	4058	4511	4987	5443	5872	6172	6549	6924	7356	7799	8468	9190	9907	10856	11096	
R	0.2	0.2	0.4	0.4	2.9	6	11.5	19.4	33.2	53.6	77.2	72.5	86.7	102	119.4	137.8	156.7	175.8	196.9	220.3	244.9	271.2	298.7	327	356.9	390.9	426.7	477	554.2	
I	0.7	1.8																												
T O T A L S Cumulative non-CMEA																														
A	392	832	1114	1419	1842	2852	4055	4074	4564	5276	6409	7430	7626	8178	8792	9513	10431	11208	11889	12328	13308	13272	17795	18120	19639	25382	28584	29585	30220	
D	203	450	514	600	731	906	1163	1578	2126	2688	3301	3950	4678	5372	5992	6559	7159	7748	8343	8970	9699	10428	11458	12706	14411	16102	18008	20486	22887	
R	145	155	155	165	180	203	227	261	306	389	521	719	937	1198	1504	1843	2242	2695	3176	3698	4259	4848	5429	6008	6600	7204	7878	8554	9269	
I	24	24	26.8	30.1	33.5	39.1	47.3	58.9	77.4	105	138	181	231	286	349.9	417.4	488.7	568	653.9	749.3	848.1	943.7	1038	1135	1239	1356	1479	1621	1795	
T O T A L S Cumulative																														
A	392	832	1114	1419	1842	2852	4055	4074	4564	5276	6409	7430	7626	8178	8792	9513	10431	11208	11889	12328	13308	13272	17795	18120	19639	25382	28584	29585	30220	30220
D	203	450	514	600	731	906	1163	1578	2126	2688	3301	3950	4678	5372	5992	6559	7159	7748	8343	8970	9699	10428	11458	12706	14411	16102	18008	20486	22887	22887
R	145	450	155	165	180	203	227	261	306	389	521	719	937	1198	1504	1843	2242	2695	3176	3698	4259	4848	5429	6008	6600	7204	7878	8554	9269	9269
I	24	24	26.8	30.1	33.5	39.1	47.3	58.9	77.4	105	138	181	231	286	349.9	417.4	488.7	568	653.9	749.3	848.1	943.7	1038	1135	1239	1356	1479	1621	1795	1795

D = Includes previous years

GRAND TOTALS
IN CURRENT $US

This table differs from the previous table only in that disbursements have been converted into current $US by factoring after 1971 (see table 2 on p. xxi). It is reproduced so that direct comparisons can be made with the contributions of other aid donors. It is also used as the base for calculating Soviet economic aid in constant prices—see the following table.

TOTALS		55	56	57	58	59	60	61	62	63	64	65	66	67	68	69	70	71	72	73	74	75	76	77	78	79	80	81	82	83	55-83
CMEA Countries	A		225D	61			200	500		16	41	872		33		188	644		11	380	79	68	3199	111	153	254	3653	2575	284	220	13767
	D		215D	9	23	23	21	67	150	165	146	212	243	270	232	158	114	124	145.4	199.4	357.3	391	358.7	602	861.2	1138	1068	1155	1454	1363	11265
	R		145D	10	10	10	10	10	14	20	20	17	59.3	62.6	68.6	87.3	91.5	126.7	135.9	140.4	140.5	141.7	183.7	185	176.3	174.8	173.8	221.8	218.6	218.5	2873
	I		24D	2	2	2	2.5	2.7	3.7	4.7	7	9.9	11.4	14.2	15.1	17.6	18.4	18.9	19.1	21.1	23.4	24.6	26.3	27.5	28.3	29.9	34	35.8	50.3	77.2	554.2
non-CMEA Countries	A	392D	215	221	305	423	810	703	19	474	671	262	1021	163	552	425.5	493.7	471	796.3	300.7	360	812.6	864.3	412	172.9	1265	2090	627	716.9	415	16453
	D	203D	32	55	63	108	154	190	264	383	416	401	406	458	462	461.1	453.7	475.9	496.8	514.1	346.8	440.8	415.2	464.7	514.7	764.4	800.7	722.1	911.8	875.7	12255
	R		0.2	0.2	0.2	5	13	13.6	20.1	25.1	62.8	115	139	156	193	218	247.7	272.7	316.7	340.5	382	419.1	405.7	395.7	402.7	416.9	430.5	452.6	457.2	496.2	6396
	I		0.7	0.7	1.1	1.1	3.1	5.5	7.9	13.8	20.4	23.6	30.8	35.9	40.7	45.9	49.1	52.4	60.2	64.8	72	74.2	69.3	66.4	68.7	74.5	82.6	87.4	92.2	96.8	1241
All Countries	A	392D	440D	282	305	423	1010	1203	19	490	712	1134	1021	196	552	613.5	1138	471	807.3	680.7	439	880.6	4063	523	325.9	1519	5743	3202	1001	635	30220
	D	203D	247D	64	86	131	175	257	414	548	562	613	649	728	694	619.1	567.3	599.9	642.2	713.5	704.1	831.8	773.9	1067	1376	1903	1869	1877	2365	2238	23520
	R		145D	10.2	10.2	15	23	23.6	34.1	45.1	82.8	132	198	218	261	305.3	339.2	399.4	452.6	480.9	522.5	560.8	589.4	580.7	579	591.7	604.3	674.4	675.8	714.7	9269
	I		24D	2.8	3.3	3.4	5.6	8.2	11.6	18.5	27.4	33.5	42.2	50.1	55.8	63.5	67.5	71.3	79.3	85.9	95.4	98.8	95.6	93.9	97	104.4	116.6	123.2	142.5	174	1795
Cumulative CMEA	A		225D	286	286	286	486	986	986	1002	1043	1915	1915	1948	1948	2136	2780	2780	2791	3171	3250	3318	6517	6628	6781	7035	10688	13263	13547	13767	
	D		215D	224	247	270	291	358	508	673	819	1031	1274	1544	1776	1934	2048	2172	2317	2517	2874	3265	3624	4226	5087	6225	7293	8449	9902	11265	
	R		145D	155	165	175	185	195	209	229	249	266	325	388	457	543.8	635.3	762	897.9	1038	1179	1321	1504	1689	1866	2040	2214	2436	2655	2873	
	I		24D	26.1	28.3	30.6	33.1	35.8	39.5	44.2	51.2	61.1	72.5	86.7	102	119.4	137.8	156.7	175.8	196.9	220.3	244.9	271.2	298.7	327	356.9	390.9	426.7	477	554.2	
Cumulative non-CMEA	A	392D	607	828	1133	1556	2366	3069	3088	3562	4233	4494	5515	5678	6230	6656	7150	7621	8417	8718	9078	9890	10755	11167	11339	12604	14694	15321	16038	16453	
	D	203D	235	290	353	461	615	805	1070	1453	1869	2270	2676	3134	3596	4058	4511	4987	5484	5998	6345	6785	7201	7665	8180	8944	9745	10467	11379	12255	
	R		0.2	0.2	0.4	5.4	18.4	32	52.1	77.2	140	255	393	549	742	959.7	1207	1480	1797	2137	2519	2938	3344	3740	4143	4559	4990	5443	5900	6396	
	I		0.7	0.7	1.8	2.9	6	11.5	19.4	33.2	53.6	77.2	108	144	185	230.5	279.6	332	392.2	457	529	603.2	672.5	738.9	807.6	882.1	964.7	1052	1144	1241	
Cumulative	A	393D	832	1114	1419	1842	2852	4055	4074	4564	5276	6409	7430	7626	8178	8792	9930	10401	11208	11889	12328	13208	17272	17795	18120	19639	25382	28584	29585	30220	
	D	203D	450	514	600	731	906	1163	1578	2126	2688	3301	3950	4678	5372	5992	6559	7159	7801	8514	9219	10050	10824	11891	13267	15170	17039	18916	21281	23520	
	R		155	155	165	180	203	227	261	306	389	521	719	937	1198	1504	1843	2242	2695	3176	3698	4259	4848	5429	6008	6600	7204	7878	8554	9269	
	I		24D	26.8	30.1	33.5	39.1	47.3	58.9	77.4	105	138	181	231	286	349.9	417.4	488.7	568	653.9	749.3	848.1	943.7	1038	1135	1239	1356	1479	1621	1795	

GRAND TOTALS
IN CONSTANT 1967 PRICES

After modifying the current $US prices of the previous table according to the factors published by the US Bureau of Labor Statistics (see table iii on p. xxi), this table shows Soviet agreements, disbursements, repayments, and interest in constant 1967 prices. It therefore shows the trends and fluctuations of Soviet economic development assistance for the period 1955–1983. They are illustrated by the following histograms of agreements and gross and net disbursements.

		55	56	57	58	59	60	61	62	63	64	65	66	67	68	69	70	71	72	73	74	75	76	77	78	79	80	81	82	83	55-83
TOTALS CMEA Countries	A	266D	255D				219	546		17.3	43.9	917		33		173.9	569.3		9.1	295.3	54.7	42.8	1894	61.8	79.7	120.4	1538	968.2	100.5	76.1	8096
	D	245D	293D	10	26	25	23	73	163	179	157	223	248	270	231	146.2	100.8	105.6	120.4	154.9	247.2	245.7	212.4	335.3	448.7	539.6	449.6	434.4	514.6	471.4	6408
	R	172D	172D	11.4	11.1	11.1	11	10.9	15.2	21.6	21.4	17.9	60.5	62.6	68.3	80.8	80.9	107.9	112.5	109.1	97.2	89.1	108.8	103	91.9	82.9	73.2	83.4	77.4	75.6	1868
	I	28D	28D	2.4	2.5	2.6	2.7	2.9	4	5.1	7.5	10.4	11.6	14.2	15	16.3	16.3	16.1	15.8	16.4	16.2	15.5	15.6	15.3	14.7	14.2	14.3	13.5	17.8	26.7	354.0
TOTALS non-CMEA Countries	A	208	451	322	340	470	889	767	20.5	511	718	275	1042	163	550	393.6	436.4	401.3	659.3	233.6	249.1	511.1	511.7	229.5	90.1	599.5	879.9	235.8	253.8	143.6	12555
	D			62.8	70.2	120	169	208	286	413	445	422	415	458	460	426.5	400.7	405.5	411.4	399.5	240	277.3	245.8	258.8	268.2	362.3	337.1	271.5	322.8	303	8744
	R			0.2	0.2	5.5	14.3	14.7	21.8	27.1	67.2	121	141	156	192	201.7	219	232.3	262.2	264.6	264.3	263.6	240.2	220.4	209.8	197.6	181.2	170.2	161.8	171.7	4022
	I			0.8	1.2	1.2	3.4	6	8.6	14.9	21.8	24.8	31.4	35.9	40.5	42.5	43.4	44.6	49.8	50.3	49.8	46.7	41	37	35.8	35.3	34.8	32.9	32.6	33.5	800.7
TOTALS All Countries	A	474D	521	322	340	470	1108	1313	20.5	528	762	1193	1042	196	550	567.5	1006	401.3	668.4	528.9	303.8	554	2405	291.3	169.8	719.9	2418	1204	354	219.7	20651
	D			73.1	95.8	145	192	281	449	592	602	645	663	728	691	572.7	501.5	511.1	531.8	554.4	487.3	523.2	458.2	594.1	716.9	902	786.7	706	837	774.4	15152
	R	172D		11.6	11.4	16.6	25.2	25.8	37	48.7	88.6	139	202	218	260	282.4	299.9	340.3	374.8	373.7	361.6	352.7	348.9	323.4	301.7	280.5	254.4	253.6	239	247	5890
	I	28D		3.2	3.7	3.8	6.1	9	12.6	20	29.3	35.2	43.1	50.1	55.6	58.7	59.7	60.7	65.7	66.7	66	62.1	56.6	52.3	50.5	49.5	49.1	46.3	50.4	60.2	1155
TOTALS Cumulative CMEA	A	266D	336	336	336	336	556	1102	1102	1119	1163	2080	2080	2113	2113	2287	2856	2856	2865	3161	3215	3258	5152	5214	5293	5414	6952	7920	8020	8096	
	D	245D	255	265	291	316	339	412	575	753	909	1132	1380	1650	1881	2027	2129	2234	2354	2509	2756	3002	3215	3550	3998	4538	4988	5422	5936	6408	
	R	172D	172	183	195	205	217	227	242	264	286	303	364	427	495	575	656	764	877	986	1083	1172	1281	1384	1476	1558	1632	1715	1793	1868	
	I	28D	28	30.8	33.3	35.8	38.6	41.5	45.5	50.6	58.1	68.5	80.1	94.3	109	125.7	141.9	158	173.8	190.2	206.4	221.9	237.5	252.8	267.5	281.7	296	309.5	327.3	354	
TOTALS Cumulative non-CMEA	A	208	659	981	1321	1791	2680	3447	3467	3978	4696	4971	6014	6177	6727	7120	7557	7958	8617	8851	9100	9611	10123	10352	10442	11042	11922	12158	12411	12555	
	D	245D	283	346	416	536	705	913	1199	1613	2058	2480	2895	3353	3813	4240	4640	5046	5457	5857	6097	6374	6620	6879	7147	7509	7846	8118	8441	8744	
	R			0.2	0.4	5.9	20.2	34.9	56.7	83.8	151	272	413	569	761	962.6	1182	1414	1676	1941	2205	2469	2709	2929	3139	3337	3518	3688	3850	4022	
	I			0.8	2	3.2	6.6	12.6	21.2	36.1	57.9	82.8	114	150	191	233.1	276.5	321.2	371	421.3	471.2	517.8	558.9	595.9	631.6	667	701.7	734.6	767.2	800.7	
TOTALS Cumulative (All)	A	474D	995	1317	1657	2127	3235	4548	4568	5097	5859	7051	8094	8290	8840	9407	10413	10814	11483	12011	12315	12869	15275	15566	15736	16456	18873	20077	20432	20651	
	D	245D	538	611	707	852	1044	1325	1774	2366	2967	3612	4275	5003	5694	6267	6769	7280	7811	8366	8853	9376	9835	10429	11145	12047	12834	13540	14377	15152	
	R	172D	172	183	195	211	237	262	299	348	437	575	777	996	1256	1538	1838	2178	2553	2927	3288	3641	3990	4313	4615	4895	5150	5403	5643	5890	
	I	28D	28	31	35	39	45	54	66	86	116	151	194	244	300	358.8	418.4	479.2	544.8	611.6	677.6	739.7	796.3	848.6	899.2	948.7	997.8	1044	1095	1155	

D = includes previous years

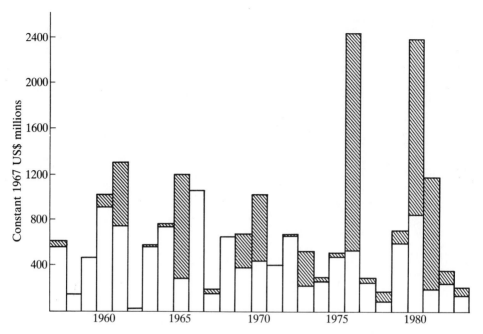

Totals of New Soviet Economic Co-operation Agreements With LDCs, 1957–1983

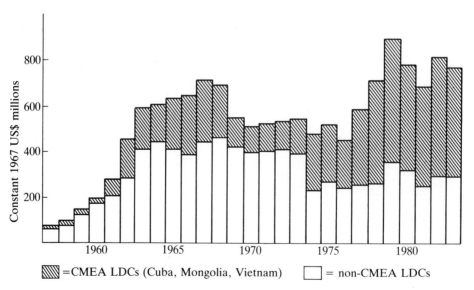

▨ =CMEA LDCs (Cuba, Mongolia, Vietnam)   ☐ = non-CMEA LDCs

Totals of Soviet Economic Aid Disbursements to the LDCs, 1957–1983

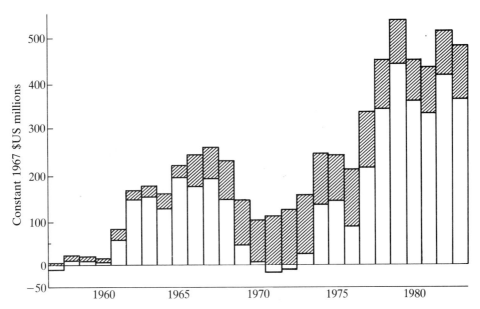

Gross Disbursement and Net Transfer of Soviet Economic Aid to CMEA Member LDCs, 1957–1983

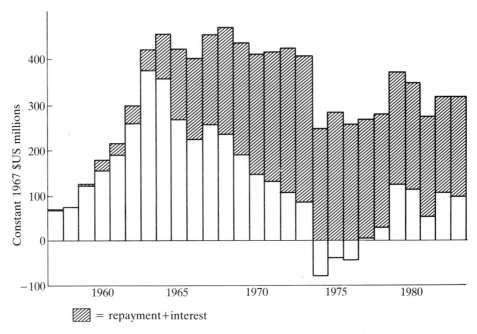

Gross Disbursement and Net Transfer of Soviet Economic Aid to Non-CMEA Member LDCs, 1957–1983

AFGHANISTAN

It was in Afghanistan that the Soviet Union started its official foreign aid programme. As early as 1921, one million gold roubles was lent for the purchase of military equipment and some services, and in 1927 the Russians supplied their southern neighbour with a radio telegraph and cotton gin; a further cotton gin was added in 1938. (Soviet aid rendered before 1954 is not included in these tables.) It was again Afghanistan that became, with North Korea, one of the first beneficiaries of the new Soviet aid programme which began after Stalin's death. In 1954 it was agreed that the Russians would provide the Afghans with a loan to help finance a number of new projects under Afghanistan's first Five Year Plan (March 1954 to March 1959). Although mainly connected with agricultural development, the projects financed by it included Afghanistan's first automobile repair shop at Djangalak, small hydro-electric projects, oil storage, and airports; the first prospecting was also started for a road through the Hindu Kush. In addition, the Soviet Union agreed to grant an interest-free loan in July 1957 for oil prospecting in northern Afghanistan. They had thus committed themselves to about $120m in foreign aid between 1954 and the end of Afghanistan's first Five Year Plan.

In addition, they agreed in May 1959 to provide grant aid of $80m for the building of the 750 kilometre Kush–Kandahar highway, including the Salang tunnel, although the agreement was not finalized until 1961. Two new loans were agreed in October 1961 to finance a number of projects included in Afghanistan's second Five Year Plan (1962 to 1967). These included geological prospecting for oil, natural gas, and minerals, the laying of a gas pipeline, the construction of an oil refinery, road building, and power generation. An additional credit was provided during this plan period for the exploitation of natural gas deposits in northern Afghanistan (October 1963). The principle and interest on this loan were to be repaid by the delivery of natural gas (1.5 billion cubic metres of gas a year) from 1966 to 1985. A gas pipeline to the Soviet border was finally installed in 1967.

One of the major projects financed out of the Soviet loan for Afghanistan's third Five Year Plan (1967 to 1972) was the development of the Shibarghan gas deposits in northern Afghanistan. The loan included a ten-year goods credit of up to 17m roubles at 2% interest to help meet local costs. Meanwhile, Afghanistan had delivered a total of

Note A: 1954.

Item		T	55	56	57	58	59	60	61	62	63	64	65	66	67	68	69	70	71	72	73	74	75	76	77	78	79	80	81	82	83	55–83
General development A = 1954	*A	28	4 A																													4
	D			2																												4
	R	3 + 5					0.8	0.8	0.8	0.8	0.8																					4.0
	I	3					0.1	0.1	0.1	0.1																						0.4
	LO				0																											
Road building A = 1954	*A	29	2 A																													2
	D			1																												.2
	R	8			0.2	0.2	0.2	0.2	0.2	0.3	0.3	0.3																				2
	I	2			0.1	0.1	0.1	0.1	0.1																							0.2
	LO				0																											
Agreement on co-op. in dev'ment of Afghan economy and offer of a credit for this	A	64		100																												100
	D				5	10	15	15	15	15	10	10	5																			100
	R	8 +22								1	1	2	2	1	1	1	1	1	4	4	4	4	4	4	4	4	4	4	5	5	55
	I	2											5	0	1	1	1	1	1	1	1	1	1	1	1	1	1	1	1	1	23
	LO				100	95	85	70	55	40	25	15	5	0																		
Oil prospecting	*A	96			15																											15
	D							3	3	3	3	3																				15
	R	25+25																														
	I	–																														
	LO	–			15	15	15	12	9	6	3	0																				
Kushka-Herat-Kandahar Road	*A	100					80																									80
	D	–																														80
	R	–										10	10	10	10	10	10	5														
	I																															
	LO							80	80	75	65	55	45	35	25	15	10	5	0													
Agreement on economic and technical co-op'n for the 2nd Five Year Plan	A	47							197																							197
	D									7	10	20	30	50	50	15	10	5														197
	R	12												1	2	2	3	3	16	16	16	16	16	16	17	17	17	17	17	5	5	197
	I	24													2	2	2	3	3	3	3	3	3	3	3	2	2	2	2	2	40
	LO									197	190	180	160	130	80	30	15	5	0													

8.8 billion cubic metres of natural gas to the Soviet Union during the period of 1967 to 1971.

In July 1972 the Soviet Union further agreed to extend a loan of 100m roubles at 2% interest for more than fifteen development projects during Afghanistan's fourth Five Year Plan (1972 to 1977). Included among the projects were the construction of an oil refinery, geological prospecting, and the building of motor roads. Three new credits were provided in February 1975 consequent upon the revolution and the declaration of the Republic of Afghanistan. They were respectively for canals and dams; for transport, communications, electric power transmission, and chemical fertilizer manufacture; and for the development of the Jarquduk natural gas field near the Soviet border in northern Afghanistan, and the textile and food industries.

In June 1976, a 660 metre raised gas pipeline was laid over the border river of Amu Darya. In August that year a second natural gas agreement was signed between the two countries to develop further gas deposits in Afghanistan. In April 1977 the Soviet Union offered further assistance to Afghanistan in the development of the gas, oil, and petrochemical industry, and many other projects, but no amounts or terms were made public. After the April revolution in 1978 the Soviets concluded a series of agreements and contracts concerning oil and gas development, power generation, copper mining, the textile industry, and transport. In March 1979 the Russians agreed to help in the creation of a mining complex based on the Ainak copper ore field from 1979 to 1984: a loan of 200m roubles at 2% interest was to be provided. They also agreed to grant a loan to help finance the construction of an oil refinery with an annual processing capacity of 500,000 tons of crude, power transmission, and other projects. In August of the same year it was agreed that the Soviet Union would help Afghanistan in the creation of seven agricultural equipment and tractor projects during the period of 1979 to 1982. 1979 saw the completion of the processing plant at the Jarquduk gas field and the start of gas extraction. The USSR promised another loan in December 1980, a year after its forces entered Afghanistan.

According to the Soviet news agancy TASS in February 1981, more than 70 development projects had been completed in Afghanistan with Soviet help. The Afghan news agency Bakhtar reported (27 January 1982) that from 1956 to 1981 more than $1,955m had been granted by the Soviet Union for various projects and the import of consumer goods, and $347m had been granted to finance technical training and other assistance. The discrepancies can lie in the calculation of the exchange rate and in the inclusion in Soviet calculations of gifts of such things as hospital and educational equipment and of deliveries that are not under 'aid' terms. Soviet annual statistics of deliveries seem a closer

		T	55	56	57	58	59	60	61	62	63	64	65	66	67	68	69	70	71	72	73	74	75	76	77	78	79	80	81	82	83	55-83
Agreement on extension of econ'c co-op'n for winning and use of natural gas	A	44									39																					39
	D																															39
	R	20										9	10	10	10	2	2	2	2	2	2	2	2	2	2	2	2	2	2	2	33
	I	24										39	30	20	10	0.5	0.5	0.5	0.5	0.5	0.5	0.5	0.5	0.5	0.5	0.5	0.5	0.5	0.5	0.5	9.0
	LO												29	26	21	16	11	6	2	0												
Road paving	*A	29										29																				29
	D												•																			29
	R	8											3	5	5	5	5	4	4	3	3	4	4	4	4	4						29
	I	2															0.1	0.4	0.4	0	0.3	0.3	0.3	0.3	0.3	0.3						3.0
	LO												29	26	21	16	11	6	2													
2nd Protocol to Agr't on technical co-op'n for the exploit'n of Kabul Housing Combine	A	36										6																				6
	D																															6
	R	3 + 7															0.7	0.7	0.7	0.7	0.7	0.7	0.8									5.0
	I	2													0.1		0.1	0.1		0.1		0.1										0.5
	LO														4	2	0															
Agreement on economic and technical co-operation (i)	A	36														16	16															16
	D																															16
	R	3 + 7															2	5	5	3	1			2	2	2	2	2	3	3		16
	I	2																		0.1	0.2	0.2	0.2	0.2	0.2	0.2	0.1	0.1	0.1	0.1		1.7
	LO															16	16	14	9	4	1	0										
Agreement on economic and technical co-operation (ii)	A	44														72	72															72
	D																															72
	R	3 +12																					5	6	6	6	6	6	6	6	6	48
	I	2																	0.1	0.3	0.4	0.8	0.8	0.8	0.8	0.8	0.8	0.8	0.8	0.8	0.8	8.8
	LO																72	65	55	40	25	15	5	0								
Agreement on economic and technical co-operation (iii)	A	36														19																19
	D																															19
	R	3 + 7																					2	3	3	3	3	3				19
	I	2																		0.2	0.2	0.2	0.2	0.2	0.2	0.2	0.2	0.2	0.2			2.0
	LO																19	10	0													

match; they include also deliveries not on 'aid' terms, but exclude the personnel element in loans.

The first two Soviet credits in 1954 did not appear in the official Collection of Soviet Treaties—nor did the agreements on oil prospecting (1957), the Kush–Herat–Kandahar road (1959), the 1964 road paving agreement, and the 1968 dam and irrigation agreement, although the first general agreement for the loan of $100m did appear in that series. The pre-1965 agreements were well documented in the press at the time, and reproduced in Goldman and Müller; and the 1968 agreement was shown in the Friedrich–Ebert–Stiftung series.

Project		T	55	56	57	58	59	60	61	62	63	64	65	66	67	68	69	70	71	72	73	74	75	76	77	78	79	80	81	82	83	55–83
Dam and irrigation system near Sardeh	A	29														7																7
	D																2	3	2													7
	R	8																		1	1	1	1	1	1	1						7
	I	2																0.1	0.1	0.1	0.1	0.1	0.1	0.1								0.7
	LO																7	5	2	0												
Completion of projects and new starts	+A	44																		97												97
	D																				10	10	15	20	20	10	5	5	2			97
	R	3 +12																													8	24
	I	2																						1	1	1	1	1	1	1	1	8
	LO																			97	97	87	77	62	42	22	12	7	2	0		
Suppliers' credit	+A	36																		24												24
	D																				10	10	4									24
	R	3 + 7																								3	3	3	3	4	4	20
	I	2																				0.1		0.3	0.3	0.3	0.3	0.3	0.3	0.2	0.2	2.6
	LO																			24	24	14	4	0							
Agreement on development of economic and technical co-operation (i)	A	64																					149									149
	D																							5	15	25	30	30				99
	R	8 +22																														
	I	2																							0.4		1.0	1.5	1.5	1.5	1.6	7.5
	LO																							149	144	129	104	74	74	69	59	50
Agreement on development of economic and technical co-operation (ii)	A	44																					131									131
	D																							5	10	20	30	30				131
	R	3 +12																												3	8	16
	I	2																									0.3	0.7	1.3	1.4	1.5	1.5	6.7
	LO																							131	126	116	96	66	36	16	6	0
Agreement on development of economic and technical co-operation (iii)	A	25																						145								145
	D																								25	25	30					100
	R	8																										5	9	9	12	44
	I	3																										2	2	2	2	2	13
	LO																							145	140	125	100	70	70	65	55	45

		T	55	56	57	58	59	60	61	62	63	64	65	66	67	68	69	70	71	72	73	74	75	76	77	78	79	80	81	82	83	55-83
Agreement on economic and technical co-operation (i)	A	36																									306					306
	D																											5	20	90	120	235
	R	12																													10	10
	I	2																											0.5	1.0	1.5	3.0
	LO																											306	301	281	191	71
Agreement on economic and technical co-operation (ii)	A	44																									107					107
	D																											8	15	25	25	73
	R	3 +12																														
	I	2																											0.2	0.3	0.5	1.0
	LO																											107	99	84	59	34
Agreement on econ'c and tech'l co-operation	A	32																										308				308
	D																													50	50	100
	R	2 +10																														
	I	3																													1.0	1.0
	LO																											308	308	308	258	208
TOTALS	A		6	100	15		80		197							114				121			425				413	308	308	308	258	1853
	D		3	3	5	10	18	18	23	35	33	49	60	77	77	30	40	37	24	18	31	30	24	35	60	80	95	48	67	195	220	1445
	R				0.2	0.2	1.0	1.0	1.1	1.1	1.1	0.3		2.5	1.0	2.0	2.7	18.7	25.7	26.7	26.7	29.7	29.8	38.0	39.0	42.0	42.0	46.0	56.0	42.0	55.0	529.0
	I				0.2	0.1	0.1	0.1	0.1		2.0	2.0	1.0		3.6	3.5	4.7	5.1	5.3	5.6	5.7	6.3	6.4	7.3	8.4	9.0	9.6	10.7	11.3	9.9	11.6	132.1
	LO			3	100	110	100	162	144	318	283	289	275	215	138	61	145	105	68	44	147	116	86	487	452	392	312	630	890	823	628	408
Soviet Foreign Trade Statistics	D		1.0	1.7	3.3	9.7	14.7	17.4	18.6	19.3	23.9	27.8	29.9	45.0	28.6	18.1	71.6	25.6		20.4	14.6	14.1	22.5	28.1	44.3	73.6	88.1	96.8	97.1	95.1	90.4	1041

ALGERIA

The first agreement, signed in September 1963, was a general credit, and the projects to be built were to be the subject of later agreements. This accounts for the long period of expenditure. Under this credit projects included a training institute, vocational schools, minerals prospecting, irrigation, and the provision of agricultural equipment and commercial aircraft. This was supplemented by a further loan in 1966. The other agreements with Algeria were for the specific projects at Annaba and M'Sila. The first stage of the Annaba iron and steel works was opened in 1969, the second in 1980; the completion of the aluminium works at M'Sila was also apparently achieved about 1980.

The increase in Soviet deliveries shown in the Soviet foreign trade statistics can be attributed to two new agreements of April 1980 and January 1981, but their terms (at 7% interest with repayment over three years with one year's grace) represent a grant element of only 6%, and therefore do not come into the 'aid' category.

All agreements were published in the Soviet Treaty series.

Agreement / item	T	55	56	57	58	59	60	61	62	63	64	65	66	67	68	69	70	71	72	73	74	75	76	77	78	79	80	81	82	83	55-83
Agreement on economic and technical co-operation — A	38									100																					100
— D												2	8	10	15	15	15	10	10	8	5	2									100
— R	15																5	6	7	8	8	8	8	8	8	8	8	8	5		100
— I	2½													0.5	1.0	1.3	1.3	1.3	1.3	1.3	1.3	1.3	1.3	1.3	1.3	1.3	1.2	1.0	1.0		19.0
— LO											100	100	98	90	80	65	50	35	25	15	7	2	0								
Agr't on ext'n of econ'c and tech'l co-op'n in the construction of a steel plant — A	38										127																				127
— D													15	50	50	10	2														127
— R	15														4	7	9	9	9	9	9	9	9	9	9	9	9	9	9		127
— I	2½													1.0	1.7	1.7	1.7	1.7	1.7	1.7	1.7	1.7	1.7	1.7	1.7	1.7	1.7	1.7	1.7		26.0
— LO												127	127	112	62	12	2	0													
Protocol to the Agr't on econ'c and tech'l co-op'n on dev't of some branches of ind'y — A	38											12																			12
— D														3	3	3	3														12
— R	15															0.8	0.8	0.8	0.8	0.8	0.8	0.8	0.8	0.8	0.8	0.8	0.8	0.8	0.8	0.8	12.0
— I	2½													0.1	0.1	0.2	0.2	0.2	0.2	0.2	0.2	0.2	0.1	0.1	0.1	0.1	0.1	0.1	0.1	0.1	2.5
— LO																															
Agree't on co-op'n in construction of 2nd stage of steel plant at El Hadjar (Annaba) — A	38																	190													190
— D																			10	20	20	50	50	20	10	10					190
— R	15																						8	13	13	13	13	13	13	13	99
— I	2½																				1.2	2.0	2.6	2.6	2.6	2.6	2.6	2.6	2.6	2.6	24.0
— LO																			190	180	160	140	90	40	20	10	0				
Agree't on co-op'n in construction of an aluminium plant at M'sila — A	31																						320								320
— D																								50	50	70	60	50	40		320
— R	3+10																										5	10	20	32	67
— I	4																									1.7	4.6	6.9	6.9	6.9	27.0
— LO																							320	320	270	220	150	90	40	0	

	T	55	56	57	58	59	60	61	62	63	64	65	66	67	68	69	70	71	72	73	74	75	76	77	78	79	80	81	82	83	55-83
T A										100	127	12						190					320								749
O D													26	63	68	28	17	10	20	28	25	52	50	70	60	80	60	50	40		749
T R															6.0	10.8	14.8	15.8	16.8	17.8	17.8	17.8	25.8	30.8	30.8	30.8	35.8	40.8	46.8	45.8	405.0
A I														1.6	2.9	3.2	3.2	3.2	3.2	3.2	4.4	5.2	5.7	5.7	5.7	7.4	10.2	12.3	11.8	9.6	98.5
L S LO											100	227	237	211	148	80	52	35	215	195	167	142	90	360	290	230	150	90	40	0	
Soviet Foreign Trade Statistics D										0.6	2.0	5.9	1.7	2.9	13.8	26	17.1		23	27	27	54	78	71	61	63	50	14	57	94	689

ANGOLA

The first agreement with Angola was signed in 1976; it was for the provision over five years of medical and technical assistance, including the possibility of co-operation in energy and shipbuilding. Repayments were to be made in convertible currency. In 1979 an agreement was signed on co-operation; the terms were the same as the 1976 agreement, and since no amount was mentioned it is assumed that the credit under the 1976 agreement covered these costs. The terms of the 1982 agreement for the building of a dam, a hydro-electric power station, and an irrigation network covering 400,000 hectares on the river Cuanza were divided into two: deliveries of equipment or completion of construction were repayable over ten years starting three years after completion, whereas the provision of experts during 1982 to 1985 was to be repaid starting in the fifth year after signature (i.e. from September 1982). The agreements have not been differentiated in the tables since the necessary changes would not be significant, although the average cost of experts is estimated at about 40% of the total costs. In the 1982 Agreement it was stipulated that repayment would take place during the period 1986–95.

Both agreements were in the Soviet Treaty series.

		T	55	56	57	58	59	60	61	62	63	64	65	66	67	68	69	70	71	72	73	74	75	76	77	78	79	80	81	82	83	55-83
Protocol to Agreement on economic and technical co-operation	A	36																						40								40
	D																									3	5	10	10	8	4	40
	R	3 +10																													4	4
	I	3																										0.2	0.3	0.5	0.5	1.5
	LO																								40	40	37	32	22	12	4	0
Agr't on econ'c and technical co-operation on construction of an HEP at Kapanda	A	36																												207		207
	D																														30	30
	R	3 +10																														
	I	3																													1	1
	LO																														207	177
T O T A L S	A																							40						207		247
	D																									3	5	10	10	8	34	70
	R																														4	4
	I																											0.2	0.3	0.5	1.5	2.5
	LO																								40	40	37	32	22	12	211	177
Soviet Foreign Trade Statistics	D																									6.5	8.5	5.5	16.5	7.1	10.0	54.1

ARGENTINA

Over the decades Argentina has had a trade surplus with the Soviet Union, which buys large quantities of Argentinian grain and meat. In order to redress this imbalance somewhat the Soviet Union has offered trade credits on very advantageous terms, which for some time were better than 25% grant element. The first such Soviet credit, in 1958, was mainly intended for the supply of Soviet equipment for the development of the Argentinian oil industry, although the 1960 credit of $50m was to cover purchases on a much wider basis. The evidence for the conclusion in the table that none of these credits were taken up before 1964 and little thereafter comes from the Soviet export statistics. A new credit was agreed in 1974; it incorporated the residue (estimated in the table at $139m) of the first two credits, but the terms—at $4\frac{1}{2}\%$ with repayment in ten years—take the concessionality down to 23%, below the 'aid' standard.

The major Soviet-assisted economic development operation has been the turbines for the Salto Grande hydro-electric project on the River Uruguay, but the credit terms also fell below 25% grant element.

All agreements were included in the Soviet Treaty series.

Note B: The 1958 and 1960 credits are carried in the table only until they were incorporated in the 1974 $500m agreement, not shown in the table since it was not on 'aid' terms. The figure of $11m shown as an 'agreement' in 1975 is only the *de facto* drawing on the two agreements to rectify the totals.

	T	55	56	57	58	59	60	61	62	63	64	65	66	67	68	69	70	71	72	73	74	75	76	77	78	79	80	81	82	83	55-83
A	34				100B		50 B																								11
D											0.2	0.2	1.8	1.5	0.5	0.4	0.3	0.4	0.5	3.3	1.9	11	)	Credit transferred							11.0
R	3 + 7													0.1	0.2	0.2	0.5	0.5	0.5	0.5	0.5		)	to new credit under							3.0
I	24												0.1			0.1	0.1	0.1	0.1	0.1	0.1		)	revised, non-aid terms.							0.6
LO						100	100	150	150	150	150	150	150	148	146	146	145	145	145	144	141	139	)								

Trade credit
and
extension

BANGLADESH

The only project built by the Soviet Union in East Pakistan was a machine-tool factory at Joydevpur, designed to meet the needs of the whole of Pakistan, and almost completed by 1971. Some sources believed that the debt for Soviet assistance was written off after Bangladeshi independence, although an item of 13m roubles ($15m) does appear in official Bangladeshi statistics as a carry-over debt to the Soviet Union.

There were two inter-Governmental economic agreements in 1972 and 1975. The first, for 43m roubles, covered the construction of the first two (55 MW) units of the Ghorasal natural gas power station, which were commissioned in 1974 and 1975, broadcasting transmitters, an electrical engineering plant at Chittagong (originally conceived to complement a heavy electrical engineering plant at Taxila, between Islamabad and Peshawar, which was not built), and oil and gas prospecting. The second, for 35m roubles, covered further oil and gas prospecting and prospecting for minerals, but five other projects proposed in it were cancelled at Bangladeshi request.

The next two agreements were signed by the Soviet Tekhnopromeksport, a subsidiary of the GKES, and the Bangladeshi Power Development Board, for the construction of the third and fourth units (210MW each) of the Ghorasal power station; both agreements were signed in 1981, but the contracts were signed in 1981 and 1983 respectively. Construction of the third unit had just started in 1983, and the Soviet delivery figures have been taken as reflecting the export from the USSR rather than the deliveries in Ghorasal.

The first two agreements were published in the Soviet Treaty series. Many sources spoke of the further developments in Ghorasal, the most complete perhaps being the Soviet pamphlet published in 1983 in Dhaka—*Decade of Fruitful Co-operation: 1972–1982*, supplemented by the Soviet representative there.

Item		T	55	56	57	58	59	60	61	62	63	64	65	66	67	68	69	70	71	72	73	74	75	76	77	78	79	80	81	82	83	55-83
Agreement on	A	36																		52												52
economic	D																																52
and	R	12																							1	2	2	3	3	4	4	19
technical	I	2																						0.5	0.5	0.5	0.5	0.5	0.5	0.5	0.5	4.0
co-operation	LO																				52	50	43	37	32	26	21	16	11	6	2	0
Agreement on	A	48																					48									48
economic	D																															33
and	R	3 +15																												1	2	3
technical	I	2																									0.2	0.3	0.5	0.5	0.5	2.0
co-operation	LO																							48	48	48	46	43	38	31	23	15
Third unit	*A	44																											74			74
Ghorasal	D																														2	2
Power Station	R	6 +10																														
	I	3																														
	LO																													74	74	
Fourth unit	*A	44																													75	75
Ghorasal	D																															
Power Station	R	6 +10																														
	I	3																														
	LO																															
T O T A L S	A																			52			48						74		75	249
	D																				2	7	6	5	6	7	8	10	12	12	12	87
	R																								1	2	2	3	3	5	6	22
	I																							0.5	0.5	0.5	0.7	0.8	1.0	1.0	1.0	6.0
	LO																				52	50	43	85	80	74	67	59	49	111	99	162
Soviet	D																			0.2	3.4	5.7	2.8	2.8	2.2	6.1	4.5	3.3	4.5	2.2	37.3	75
Foreign Trade																																
Statistics																																

BENIN

A 1974 economic and cultural agreement between the USSR and Benin (formerly Dahomey) was followed in 1976 by a five-year economic co-operation agreement; it covered the fields of Soviet equipment and expertise in cartography, mineral prospecting, and training. The 4m rouble credit was raised to 5m roubles in 1978. There are no Soviet statistics giving deliveries under economic co-operation agreements, and estimates of drawings have been guided by trade deliveries, although most of the aid offered was for services.

The 1974 agreement was widely publicized in the media—for example, Marchés Tropicaux of 19 April and the East German Aussenwirtschaft No. 17 of 24 April, without any amount or terms. It was therefore presumably a framework agreement. The economic and cultural protocol was signed in November 1976, giving the figure of 4m roubles (Marchés Tropicaux of 19 November), and the increase of the credit to 5m roubles was published in the Soviet Treaty series.

		T	55	56	57	58	59	60	61	62	63	64	65	66	67	68	69	70	71	72	73	74	75	76	77	78	79	80	81	82	83	55-83
Credit	+A	43																						5.4								5.4
	D																								1.2	1.4	1.4	1.4				5.4
	R	4 +11																												0.4	0.5	0.9
	I	2½																										0.1	0.1	0.1	0.1	0.4
	LO																								5.4	4.2	2.8	1.4	0.0			
Protocol on extending economic co-op'n in founding a State Farm	A	34																								1.5						1.5
	D																											0.5	0.5	0.5		1.5
	R	12																													0.1	0.1
	I	2½																												...	...	
	LO																										1.5	1.5	1.0	0.5	0.0	
T O T A L S	A																							5.4		1.5						6.9
	D																								1.2	1.4	1.4	1.9	0.5	0.5		6.9
	R																													0.4	0.6	1.0
	I																											0.1	0.1	0.1	0.1	0.4
	LO																								5.4	4.2	4.3	2.9	1.0	0.5	0.0	

BOLIVIA

In 1968 the Bolivian president was engaged in discussions about a $100m credit for the development of the Bolivian oilfields, but it is not sure that this agreement was concluded and in any case no terms were mentioned. Two years later, in September 1970, an agreement was signed for the development of Bolivia's tin industry; the terms were $7\frac{1}{2}\%$ in advance, $7\frac{1}{2}\%$ on conclusion of contract, and the rest repayable in six-monthly tranches in US dollars. The figure of $28m was a maximum. The interest rate for the Bolivian government was 3%, but any taken up by private borrowers was to be $3\frac{1}{2}\%$ which would have lowered the grant element to 28%. Since it makes little difference, the tables arbitrarily assume that all was used at the 3% rate.

The 1970 agreement led to the construction of a volatilization plant at Potosi. Agreements were signed for further credits in 1976 (for a second volatilization plant at Potosi) and in 1982, but in these cases the terms were well below 25% grant element.

The agreement shown in the table was published in the Soviet Treaty series.

		T	55	56	57	58	59	60	61	62	63	64	65	66	67	68	69	70	71	72	73	74	75	76	77	78	79	80	81	82	83	55-83
Agreement on delivery of machinery and equipment from USSR to Bolivia	A	30																28														28
	D																				1	1	2	4	5	5	5	4	1			28
	R	1+10																						0.1	1.0	1.0	2.7	2.7	2.7	2.7	2.7	15.5
	I	3																						0.2	0.2	0.3	0.5	0.5	0.4	0.4	0.4	3.0
	LO																		28	28	27	26	24	20	15	10	5	1	0			

BURMA

In 1955 the first trade agreement was signed between the Soviet Union
and Burma, and at the same time the Soviet Union offered to grant the
equipment for a hospital, a technical institute, and a sports centre. In
1957 two development credits were agreed: the first, for the purchase
of agricultural equipment up to a value of $3.2m, was under the terms of
$2\frac{1}{2}\%$ interest and repayable in five years, bringing it below the 'aid'
·category; the second in the same agreement, and shown in the table, was
under more generous terms. The 1962 agreement was also intended to
improve irrigation. The third 'aid' agreement was announced as being to
a value of 750,000 roubles. Other economic agreements between the
two countries have been on the basis of the barter of Soviet industrial
goods for Burmese rice, and the concessionality cannot therefore be
measured.

The 1957 agreement was published in *The Times* of 10 January
1958 and in Müller; the 1962 agreement was announced by TASS on
30 August 1962; and the third agreement, in 1973, was announced by
Rangoon radio on 30 September.

Project		T	55	56	57	58	59	60	61	62	63	64	65	66	67	68	69	70	71	72	73	74	75	76	77	78	79	80	81	82	83	55-83
Irrigation equipment	*A	34			6.3																											6.3
	D						2	2	2.3																							6.3
	R	12								0.5	0.5	0.5	0.5	0.5	0.5	0.5	0.5	0.5	0.6	0.6	0.6											6.3
	I	24								0.1	0.1	0.1	0.1	0.1	0.1	0.1	0.1	0.1	0.1													1.0
	LO					6.3	6.3	4.3	2.3	0.0																							
Chemoltan irrigation network	*A	34								3.9																						3.9
	D											0.9	1	1	1																	3.9
	R	12														0.3	0.3	0.3	0.3	0.3	0.3	0.3	0.3	0.3	0.4	0.4	0.4					3.9
	I	24																0.1	0.1	0.1	0.1	0.1	0.1									0.6
	LO										3.9	3.9	3.0	2.0	1.0	0.0																
Gypsum and limestone plant Hsipa	*A	34																			1											1
	D																						0.5	0.5								1.0
	R	12																							0.2	0.2	0.2	0.2	0.1	0.1		1.0
	I	24																									0.1					0.1
	LO																				1	1	1								
T O T A L S	A				6.3					3.9											1											11.2
	D						2.0	2.0	2.3			0.9	1.0	1.0	1.0								0.5	0.5								11.2
	R									0.5	0.5	0.5	0.5	0.5	0.5	0.8	0.8	0.8	0.9	0.9	0.9	0.3	0.3	0.3	0.6	0.6	0.6	0.2	0.1	0.1		11.2
	I									0.1	0.1	0.1	0.1	0.1	0.1	0.1	0.1	0.2	0.2	0.1	0.1	0.1	0.1				0.1					1.7
	LO					6.3	6.3	4.3	2.3	0.0	3.9	3.9	3.0	2.0	1.0	0.0					1	1	1									
Soviet Foreign Trade Statistics	D										0.9	2.1	0.5	0.3																		3.8

CAMEROON

In accordance with their frequent practice in their relations with the LDCs, the Russians followed the signature of their first trade agreement with Cameroon in 1962 by the offer in the following year of a development credit. No terms were announced, but they are assumed to have been the standard terms of that time: $2\frac{1}{2}\%$ interest with twelve years to repay. The agreement is later referred to as the 1966 agreement, which may reflect some delay in ratification.

There are no Soviet records of deliveries to Cameroon under economic co-operation agreements, but some trade deliveries shown in Soviet exports may have been on 'aid' terms, and there was certainly some Soviet technical aid in the setting up of agricultural colleges and a radio transmitting station.

The agreement was originally announced by Yaoundé radio on 15 April 1966.

	T	55	56	57	58	59	60	61	62	63	64	65	66	67	68	69	70	71	72	73	74	75	76	77	78	79	80	81	82	83	55-83
*A	34									7.8																					7.8
D														0.5	0.5																1.0
R	12																0.1		0.1	0.1	0.1		0.1	0.1	0.1	0.1	0.1				1.0
I	2½																0.1					0.1									0.2
LO											7.8	7.8	7.8	7.8	7.3	6.8	6.8	6.8	6.8	6.8	6.8	6.8	6.8	6.8	6.8	6.8	6.8	6.8	6.8	6.8	6.8

Development credit

CAPE VERDE ISLANDS

The credit announced in the Soviet Treaty series was mainly for the development of the port facilities at Palmeira on Sal Island. Press and radio reports suggested that all the equipment had been delivered by 1983.

		T	55	56	57	58	59	60	61	62	63	64	65	66	67	68	69	70	71	72	73	74	75	76	77	78	79	80	81	82	83	55-83
Protocol to	A	63																									4.7					4.7
Agreement on	D																											0.5	0.5	1.0	2.7	4.7
economic and	R	5 +12																															
technical	I	-																															
co-operation	LO																											4.7	4.2	3.7	2.7	0.0

CENTRAL AFRICAN REPUBLIC

In 1968 the Russians signed an agreement on scientific, technical, and cultural co-operation with President Bokassa; in 1969 a trade agreement was signed, followed in the next year by the first economic and technical co-operation agreement. No terms were published, but they have here been assumed to be the standard Soviet co-operation terms of the period: $2\frac{1}{2}\%$ interest with twelve years to repay.

The objectives of the Soviet co-operation agreement included the construction of hydro-electric power stations, prospecting for minerals, and applications of Soviet technology to cotton growing. The 1975 credit was stated to be for further Soviet technical assistance and the establishment of a state cotton farm, but there is no evidence of any of the latter credit being taken up.

The first agreement was announced by TASS on 6 July 1970; the second was published in the Soviet Treaty series.

	T	55	56	57	58	59	60	61	62	63	64	65	66	67	68	69	70	71	72	73	74	75	76	77	78	79	80	81	82	83	55-83
Credit for *A	34																1.7														1.7
D																				0.7	0.7	0.3									1.7
feasibility R	12																						0.1	0.1	0.1	0.1	0.1	0.1	0.1	0.2	0.9
studies I	2½																					...	0.1			0.1			0.1		0.3
LO																		1.7	1.7	1.7	1.0	0.3	0.0								2.6
General A	34																					2.6									2.6
D																															
credit R	12																														
I	2½																														
LO																															
TOTALS A																	1.7					2.6	2.6	2.6	2.6	2.6	2.6	2.6	2.6	2.6	4.3
D																				0.7	0.7	0.3									1.7
R																							0.1	0.1	0.1	0.1	0.1	0.1	0.1	0.2	0.9
I																							0.1			0.1			0.1		0.3
LO																		1.7	1.7	1.7	1.0	0.3	2.6	2.6	2.6	2.6	2.6	2.6	2.6	2.6	2.6

CHAD

The 1968 credit was for the construction of a medical school and the establishment of a state organization for road construction. It was published in the Soviet Treaty series.

	T	55	56	57	58	59	60	61	62	63	64	65	66	67	68	69	70	71	72	73	74	75	76	77	78	79	80	81	82	83	55-83
A	34														2.2																2.2
D																															
R	12															0.2	1.0	1.0	0.2	0.2	0.2	0.2	0.2	0.2	0.2	0.2	0.2	0.2	0.1	0.1	2.2
I	2½																	0.1			0.1			0.1				0.1	0.1	0.1	0.4
LO																2.2	2.0	1.0	0.0												

Agreement on economic and technical co-op'n

CHILE

The Soviet Union signed a trade agreement with Chile in December 1966, and in the following month a new agreement was signed for a $42m Soviet credit for industrial development. In March 1968 a separate credit was agreed for the development of the fishing industry. Neither of these credits were taken up before 1971 because of Chilean objections to a gold clause in the repayments; but in 1971 the first Soviet fisheries experts arrived and in July 1972 the two agreements were renewed. Soon after, a new credit was awarded for the development of a fishing port in southern Chile between the provinces of Concepcion and Arauco. Diplomatic relations were suspended soon after the fall of Allende in September 1973, and no further work was done on the development projects.

The January 1967 agreement appeared in the Soviet Treaty series; the $15m agreement was carried by various sources in 1967 and early 1968, and confirmed by *Blick durch die Wirtschaft* of 26 April 1969 when mentioning the repayment problem. The renewal of the agreements came from *BfA/NfA* Annex of 17 July 1972; Prensa Latina and others published details of the $260m credit, but *BfA/NfA* of 1 August 1972 give the figure as $220m. Since little was spent the figure is immaterial. Repayments in the table are hypothetical; in practice it was likely that they were interrupted in 1973, and certainly an agreement was reached for the settlement of Chilean debts to the USSR of $31.5m in 1980 (*Latin American Weekly Report* of 5 December 1980).

Description		T	55	56	57	58	59	60	61	62	63	64	65	66	67	68	69	70	71	72	73	74	75	76	77	78	79	80	81	82	83	55-83
Credit mainly for development of fisheries industry	*A	25													15																	15
	D																		1	2	2											5
	R	8																				0.5	0.5	0.5	0.5	0.5	0.5	0.5	0.5	0.5	0.5	5.0
	I	3																			0.1	0.1	0.1	0.1	0.1	0.1	0.1	0.1	0.1	0.1	0.1	1.0
	LO	3														15	15	15	15	14	12	10	10	10	10	10	10	10	10	10	10	10
Agree't on tech'l co-op'n in const'n of industrial and other projects and ext'n of credit	A	29													42																	42
	D																				2											2
	R	10																				0.2	0.2	0.2	0.2	0.2	0.2	0.2	0.2	0.2	0.2	2.0
	I	3																				0.1				0.1				0.1		0.3
	LO															42	42	42	42	42	42	40	40	40	40	40	40	40	40	40	40	40
Credit for fisheries	*A	34																		260												260
	D																			15	5											20
	R	12																				2	2	2	2	2	2	2	2	2	2	20
	I	2½																			0.1	0.3	0.3	0.3	0.3	0.3	0.3	0.2	0.2	0.2	0.2	2.7
	LO																				245	240	240	240	240	240	240	240	240	240	240	240
TOTALS	A														57					260												317
	D																		1	17	9											27
	R																					2.7	2.7	2.7	2.7	2.7	2.7	2.7	2.7	2.7	2.7	27.0
	I																				0.2	0.5	0.4	0.4	0.4	0.5	0.4	0.3	0.3	0.3	0.3	4.0
	LO															57	57	57	57	56	299	290	290	290	290	290	290	290	290	290	290	290
Soviet Foreign Trade Statistics	D																			12.2	4.5											16.7

COLOMBIA

The first trade agreement between Colombia and the USSR was concluded in 1968. Probably because of the considerable imbalance of trade, the Soviet Union offered the Colombians credits for the purchase of Soviet machinery and equipment with a ten-year repayment period at 5%; this is not, however, eligible to be considered as aid since it falls below 25% grant element. The Russians were invited to take part in the discussions concerning the construction of two hydro-electric projects on the Sinu river; a consortium of Westinghouse, the Soviet representatives, and an international bank, and the Russians contributed a credit of $70m with repayment over ten years at $4\frac{1}{2}\%$, but this was still not on aid terms. Finally the Soviet agreement to lend $111m at £$4\frac{1}{2}\%$ over ten years with a five-year grace period does qualify (Bogota Radio, 12 July 1982); it was for part of the equipment to be supplied by the USSR for the construction of the Urra project on the Sinu, with a total estimated cost of $1.8 billion of which $1 billion was to be in foreign exchange.

Credit for first stage of Alto Sinu HEP	T	55	56	57	58	59	60	61	62	63	64	65	66	67	68	69	70	71	72	73	74	75	76	77	78	79	80	81	82	83	55-83
#A	32																												111		111
D																															
R	5 +10																														
I	4½																														
LO																														111	111

CONGO

Soviet economic co-operation with the Congo (Brazzaville) has been continuous since the first agreement in 1964—a general credit for irrigation and geological prospecting: the terms were amended in the following year to add a three-year grace period before the start of repayments. The 1973 agreement was mainly directed towards further geological prospecting. In 1975 work was agreed on the development of polymetallic ore deposits, further geological surveys, and the provision of a hospital. The 1981 credit was aimed at the development of the Yanga-Cubenza ore deposits, feasibility studies on ore concentration, and housing construction: this loan included an item of 3m roubles ($4m) for Soviet deliveries of commodities for sale to cover local costs.

All the agreements on economic co-operation between the USSR and the Congo were published in the Soviet Treaty series.

Agreement		T	55	56	57	58	59	60	61	62	63	64	65	66	67	68	69	70	71	72	73	74	75	76	77	78	79	80	81	82	83	55-83
Agreement on economic and technical co-op'n	A	34																														9.0
	D													2	1	1	1	1	1	1	1											9.0
	R	3 +12																	0.5	0.5	0.5	0.5	0.5	0.5	0.5	0.5	0.5	0.5	0.5	0.5	0.5	6.5
	I	2½														0.2	0.2	0.2	0.2	0.1	0.1	0.1	0.1	0.1	0.1	0.1	0.1	0.1	0.1	0.1	0.1	2.0
	LO											9	9	7	6	5	4	3	2	1												
Protocol to Agreement on econ'c and tech'l co-operation of 14th Dec 1964	A	41																			0.7											0.7
	D																				0.3	0.2	0.2									0.7
	R	3 +12																														0.3
	I	2½																														0.1
	LO																				0.7	0.4	0.2									
Agreement on economic and technical co-op'n	A	34																					30									30
	D																							2	5	8	8	5	2			30
	R	12																														13
	I	2½																							0.1	0.3	0.5	0.4	0.4	0.4	0.4	2.5
	LO																						30	28	23	15	7	2				
Agreement on further development of economic and technical co-op'n	A	29																											42			42
	D																													6	8	14
	R	10																														
	I																															
	LO																												42	36	28	28
T O T A L S	A											9									0.7		30						42			81.7
	D													2	1	1	1	1	1	1	1	0.3	0.2	2.2	5	8	8	5	2	6	8	53.7
	R																		0.5	0.5	0.5	0.5	0.5	0.5	0.5	0.5	0.6	2.6	3.6	3.5	3.6	19.8
	I															0.2	0.2	0.2	0.2	0.1	0.1	0.1	0.1	0.1	0.2	0.5	0.6	0.5	0.5	0.5	0.5	4.6
	LO											9	9	7	6	5	4	3	2	1	0.7	0.4	30.2	28	23	15	7	2	42	36	28	28
Soviet Foreign Trade Statistics	D												0.1	0.1	0.1	0.1	0.5	0.2										0.3	2.2	6.8	3.2	17.5

COSTA RICA

A trade agreement was signed between the USSR and Costa Rica in 1970, in which the Russians offered a trade credit on unspecified terms up to $10m. A protocol to this agreement signed in 1971 raised this credit to a minimum of $15m for the purchase of a wide range of Soviet machinery and equipment, particularly for the coffee industry. The terms were 3% interest for Costa Rican government purchases and $3\frac{1}{2}$% for purchases by private companies, but for the sake of simplicity and because separation would be difficult the tables assume a 3% rate throughout; repayment was to be over ten years in six-monthly instalments. According to Soviet foreign trade statistics their exports to Costa Rica remained very low over the next few years; this has been used as a basis for estimating the take-up of this credit, and it has been assumed that the favourable terms were granted even though the minimum was not reached.

Information on the 1970 trade agreement came from *Marktinformationen* no. 42, 1970; the 1971 agreement was contained in the Soviet Treaty series.

Protocol on delivery of machinery and equipment from USSR to Costa Rica

	T	55	56	57	58	59	60	61	62	63	64	65	66	67	68	69	70	71	72	73	74	75	76	77	78	79	80	81	82	83	55-83
A	30																	15													15
D																				0.2	0.5	0.4	0.2	...	...	0.3					1.6
R	14+10																							0.1	0.1	0.1	0.1	0.1	0.1	0.1	0.7
I	3																											0.1	0.1	0.1	0.3
LO																			15.0	15.0	14.8	14.3	13.9	13.7	13.7	13.7	13.4	13.4	13.4	13.4	13.4

CUBA

The first Soviet credit to Cuba was extended in 1960, when already the USSR was an important buyer of Cuban sugar* and continued to be so. The credit was to finance the construction of a wide range of projects: two thermal power plants, an oil refinery, a fertilizer plant, a car repair works, three metallurgical works, and housing. Two identical agreements in 1963 and 1964 on land irrigation and drainage were followed in 1965 by two agreements to extend and supplement the 1960 agreement: the first to continue the work in general and the second concentrating more specifically on geological prospecting. Two new agreements in 1965 and 1967 were for the rehabilitation and development of the sugar industry, and in 1969 and 1970 protocols extended the 1964 agreement on irrigation and the 1960 and 1965 agreements on geological prospecting respectively. Agreements on specific projects were replaced in 1973 by general credits for Cuba's Five Year Plans. The first, in 1973, was for three years only to get them into step with the Plans of the other CMEA countries.

The tables assume that all the projects were completed, or the finance allocated to them were transferred to other projects on the same terms if not, and that all the credits for the Five Year Plans were also drawn, or were being drawn in full at the end of the period. The 1973 agreement included a clause rescheduling some of Cuba's past debts, but in accordance with the policy of this paper (see page xviii) it has not been taken into account here.

All the agreements were published in the Soviet Treaty series except the 1973 agreement announced by Fidel Castro on Havana Radio on 4 January 1973, and the 1976 agreement carried by *BfA/NfA* (e) on 27 April 1976.

---

* For Soviet pricing policy towards Cuba see pp. xiv–xv.

Item	Measure	T	60	61	62	63	64	65	66	67	68	69	70	71	72	73	74	75	76	77	78	79	80	81	82	83	55-83
Agreement on offer of a credit	A	34	100																								100
	D			2	10	55	20	2	1	1	9																100
	R	12							7	7	7	7	7	7	7	9	9	9	9	2	1	1	1	1	1	1	100
	I	2½							1	1	1	0	1	1	1	1	1	1	1	1	1	1	1	1	1	1	17
	LO			100	98	88	33	13	11	10	9	0															
Agreement on co-operation in carrying out land irrigation and drainage	A	34				16																					16
	D						8	8																				16
	R	12							1.3	1.3	1.3	1.3	1.3	1.3	1.3	1.3	1.3	1.3	1.3	1.3							16
	I	2½					0.1	0.3	0.3	0.3	0.2	0.2	0.2	0.2	0.2	0.2	0.2	0.2	0.2	0.2	0.2						3.0
	LO						16	8	0																			
Agreement on further co-op'n in carrying out land irrigation and drainage	A	34					16																					16
	D							8	8																			16
	R	12								1.3	1.3	1.3	1.3	1.3	1.3	1.3	1.3	1.4	1.4	1.4	1.4						16.0
	I	2½						0.1	0.2	0.2	0.2	0.2	0.2	0.2	0.2	0.2	0.2	0.2	0.2	0.2	0.2						2.7
	LO						16	16	8	0																	
Agreement to extend a credit to Cuba	A	34							167																			167
	D								30	57	50	30																167
	R	12											14	14	14	14	14	14	14	14	14	14	14	13				167
	I	2½										30	2	2	2	2	2	2	2	2	2	1	1					24
	LO								167	137	80	30	0															
Protocol on technical co-operation in geological work	A	34						13																				13
	D								6	6	1																	13
	R	12								1	1	1	2	1	1	1	1	1	1	1	1	1	1				13
	I	2½							0.2	0.1	0.1	0.2	0.2	0.2	0.2	0.2	0.2	0.2	0.2	0.2	0.2	0.1	0.1	0.1				2.4
	LO								13	7	1	0																
Agreement on co-operation in reconstruction of Cuba's sugar industry	A	34						77																				77
	D								20	40	17																	77
	R	12								1	5	6	6	6	6	6	6	6	6	6	6	6	6				77
	I	2½								1	17																	14.0
	LO							77	57	17	0																	

		T	55	56	57	58	59	60	61	62	63	64	65	66	67	68	69	70	71	72	73	74	75	76	77	78	79	80	81	82	83	55-83
Protocol to Agreement on co-operation in reconstruction of sugar industry	A	34													33																	33
	D															13	20															33
	R	12																			3	3	3	3	3	3	3	3	3			33
	I	2½																			0.5	0.5	0.5	0.5	0.5	0.5	0.4	0.4	0.4			6.0
	LO																															
Supp'm'y Protocol to Prot'l of 1966 on tech'l co-op'n in land irrigation and drainage	A	34																2														2
	D																	2														2
	R	12																					0.2	0.2	0.2	0.2	0.2	0.2	0.2			1.8
	I	2½																				0.1	0.1					0.1	0.1			0.3
	LO																	2	2													
Supplement to 1960 credit for geol-ogical prospecting	*A	34																														11
	D																			3	3	2										11
	R	12																			1	1	1	1	1	1	1	1	1			9
	I	2½																			0.2	0.2	0.2	0.2	0.2	0.2	0.2	0.2	0.2			1.7
	LO																	11	11	8	5	2	0									
1973-76 Development credit	*A	65																			333											333
	D																					80	120	133								333
	R	25																							13	13	13	13	13	13	13	91
	I	–																														
	LO																				333	333	253	133	0							
1976-81 Development credit	*A	49																						1485								1485
	D																								185	300	400	300	200	100		1485
	R	25																											59	59	59	177
	I	2½																											10	10	10	30
	LO																								1485	1300	1000	600	300	100	0	
Agreement on economic and technical co-operation 1981-85	A	30																											2363			2363
	D																												263	430	530	1223
	R	2 +12																														
	I	4																												10	30	40
	LO																												2100	1670	1140	1140

	T	55	56	57	58	59	60	61	62	63	64	65	66	67	68	69	70	71	72	73	74	75	76	77	78	79	80	81	82	83	55-83
A							100	2		16	16	257		33		2	11			333			1485					2363			4616
D									10	55	28	18	65	104	90	50	2	3	3	3	82	120	133	185	300	400	300	463	530	530	3476
R (TOTALS)												7.0	8.3	9.6	14.6	30.6	33.6	32.7	32.7	35.7	35.8	37.0	37.0	43.0	40.6	39.2	38.2	77.2	74.0	74.0	700.8
I											1.1	1.4	1.5	3.6	3.5	4.9	5.1	5.2	5.1	5.1	5.2	5.4	5.3	5.3	5.1	3.7	3.8	10.6	20.1	40.1	141.1
LO								100	98	88	49	37	276	211	140	50	2	11	8	5	335	253	133	1485	1300	1000	600	300	2200	1670	1140
D (Soviet Foreign Trade Statistics)								2.1	11.1	58.0	35.4	16.3	12.9	30.2	71.0	89.1	69.3		22.8	36.8	84.8	124	154	196	287	420	541	453	531	520	3765

EGYPT

When Egypt signed her first economic co-operation agreement with the Soviet Union in January 1958, only North Korea, Afghanistan, and India had signed such agreements since the Second World War, and the terms had varied; this agreement, giving a credit at $2\frac{1}{2}\%$ repayable over twelve years, was to set a precedent as the standard terms, with few exceptions, for Soviet economic co-operation with the non-CMEA countries for the next fifteen years.

The first agreement was intended for the construction of, or feasibility studies on, 75 projects, including mining, an oil refinery, engineering, iron and steel, chemical and pharmaceutical plants, a shipyard, and a dry dock.

In December 1958 agreement was reached on the financing of the first stage of the Aswan High Dam—the diversionary tunnels and a canal for drainage and ultimately for the hydro-electric power; this stage was completed in May 1964. In 1960 a further agreement was signed for the completion of the project—the main body of the dam, the hydro-electric plant, and the electricity grid. The Soviet credits covered 16% of the first stage and 41% of the remaining work, accounting for 28% of the overall cost.

The Soviet credit offered in 1964 for Egypt's second Five Year Plan (1966–70) represented 10% of the total estimated investment. It was intended for the purchase of plant, equipment, and materials at world prices. Materials purchased under this agreement had a repayment period of only five years, which reduces the terms below the cut-off of 25% grant element; but it has not proved possible to winnow out such purchases and they have been ignored. Another agreement on the same date offered a credit of $66m for help in irrigation and drainage, but this too was repayable in five years and has therefore been excluded here.

The original 1958 agreement had included the start of construction of an iron and steel works at Helwan, near Cairo, with an initial capacity of 300,000 tonnes of steel per annum. The 1964 agreement included a continuous casting plant for the works, which was completed in 1969; and in 1969 a new agreement was signed for the expansion of the plant to a capacity of $1\frac{1}{2}$ million tonnes of steel, which was completed in the mid-1970s.

In 1970 a new agreement was signed for Soviet assistance in the construction of three new plants—an aluminium works at Nag Hammadi, a

Agreement	Item	T	55	56	57	58	59	60	61	62	63	64	65	66	67	68	69	70	71	72	73	74	75	76	77	78	79	80	81	82	83	55-83
Agreement on economic and technical co-operation	*A	34				175																										175
	D																															
	R	12						10	20	30	45	40	20	10	15	15	15	14	14	14	14	14	10	5								175
	I	2½							0.3	0.5	1.4	1.4	2.4	2.4	2.3	2.3	2.3	2.3	2.3	2.3	2.3	2.3	2.0	1.2								30.0
	LO						175	175	165	145	115	70	30	10	0																	
Agreements on econ'c and tech'l assistance/co-op'n in construction of Aswan High Dam	*A	34				100		225																								325
	D								10	10	20	35	45	45	40	35	30	20	20	15												325
	R	12												8	8	26	26	26	27	27	27	28	28	28	28	19	19					325
	I	2½												3	4	4	5	5	5	5	5	5	5	5	2	1	1					58
	LO						100	100	325	315	305	285	250	205	160	120	85	55	35	15	0											
General development aid supplement	*A	34									45																					45
	D																															
	R	12													2	3	4	4	4	4	4	4	4	4	4	4						45
	I	2½													0.6	0.6	0.6	0.6	0.6	0.6	0.6	0.6	0.6	0.6	0.5	0.5						7.0
	LO												45	35	15	0																
Agreement on econ'c and tech'l co-op'n for ind'l projects under the Egyptian 2nd FYP	*A	34										280																				280
	D													20	50	80	60	50	15	5												280
	R	12															10	15	20	25	25	20	25	20	20	20	20	20	15	10	10	280
	I	2½													0.5	1.0	1.5	2.0	3.5	3.8	3.8	3.8	3.8	3.8	3.8	3.8	3.8	3.8	2.0	1.8	0.5	47.0
	LO												280	280	260	210	130	70	20	5												
Agreement on construction of Helwan Iron and Steel Works	*A	34														160																160
	D																100															
	R	12																			40	20	25	10	10	5	13	13	13	13	13	104
	I	2½																		0.3	0.7	1.6	1.8	2.2	2.2	2.2	2.2	2.2	2.2	2.2	2.2	22.0
	LO															160	160	150	130	110	70	50	25	15	5	0						
Triphosphates, silicon, and Naq Hammadi Aluminium works	*A	34															100															100
	D																															
	R	12																				10	8	8	8	8	8	8	8	9		73
	I	2½																				0.5	1.4	1.4	1.4	1.4	1.4	1.4	1.3	1.3	1.3	14.0
	LO																100	100	90	65	20	5	0									

triphosphate works, and a silicon works, all taking advantage of the Aswan power.

The major development credit of 1971 was apparently utilized only at a very slow pace. Much of it had been designated for the development of light and consumer industries, but in the event the most prominent projects which have been constructed under this credit have been an oil refinery and a new iron foundry.

The agreements which were not published in the Soviet Treaty series come from Goldman and Müller (1957 and 1963); *Blick durch die Wirtschaft* of 18 May 1968 and *Neues Deutschland* of 7 June 1968 (the 1968 Helwan agreement); *Le Commerce du Levant* of 30 July 1969 for the 1969 agreement, although the Nag Hammadi aluminium plant had already been planned earlier (CTK 16 December 1968). Details of the 1971 agreement came from Cairo Radio on 17 March 1971.

		T	55	56	57	58	59	60	61	62	63	64	65	66	67	68	69	70	71	72	73	74	75	76	77	78	79	80	81	82	83	55-83
General development aid	*A	34																	417													417
	D																						10	10	15	15	10	10	10	5	5	90
	R	12																									2	4	6	8	8	28
	I	2½																									0.5	1.0	1.3	1.3	1.3	5.4
	LO																			417	417	417	417	407	397	382	367	357	347	337	332	327
TOTALS	A					275		225			45	280				160	100		417													1502
	D							10	30	40	65	75	75	95	105	115	90	80	65	65	75	45	40	20	25	20	10	10	10	5	5	1175
	R										5	10	15	23	25	44	55	59	65	70	70	71	75	78	73	64	62	45	42	39	40	1030
	I								0.3	0.5	1.4	2.4	4.4	5.4	7.4	7.9	9.4	9.9	11.4	12.2	12.9	14.3	14.6	14.2	9.9	8.9	8.9	8.4	6.8	6.6	5.3	183
	LO						275	275	490	460	420	400	605	530	435	330	375	385	305	657	592	517	472	432	412	387	367	357	347	337	332	327
Soviet Foreign Trade Statistics	D					1	16	16	35	42	48	61	86	85	81	67	56	79		80	78	86	79	69	59	39	43	40	33	30	29	1339

ETHIOPIA

The Soviet Union opened its first embassy to Ethiopia in 1956, and in 1959 Emperor Haile Selassie was the first African head of state to visit Moscow. In July 1959 the Soviet Union extended a loan of 400m roubles ($100m) for a series of projects including the construction of an oil refinery at Assab, the development of the Adola gold mines, and the construction of a chemical plant. By 1970 20m (new) roubles had been used for the oil refinery but apparently very little else.

In 1977 a fresh credit of 12m (new) roubles was offered, and in 1979 the rest of the 1959 credit was added to new credits to make a total extension of $149m. Some of this was intended for the objectives listed under the 1959 agreement, but new projects were added including grain silos, agricultural machinery repair works, fodder warehouses, and refrigeration units. The 1979 protocol was for the supply of Soviet goods for sale on the local market to cover local Soviet costs in oil and gas prospecting (no interest was payable during the grace period), and the protocol for $15m in the same year was for reconstruction. The 1980 credit of $77m was for the construction of a cement works. The two 1981 grants, of 8m roubles and $16\frac{1}{2}$m roubles, were for technical training and for equipment, personnel, an aeroplane, and a helicopter for the construction of an earth dam on the Alvero River.

The 1983 agreement for the construction of the Melkana Vakana hydro-electric project included the erection of a high tension line to Kaliti and sub-stations. The other 1983 agreement was for 32m roubles to cover local Soviet costs.

All the agreements were published in the Soviet Treaty series except the first, which was widely documented at the time (see Müller and Goldman) and frequently referred to in subsequent Ethiopian–Soviet agreements.

Note C: Since the unspent amount of the 1959 credit was transferred in 1979 to a new agreement, the $26m in the agreements line for 1978 represents only the sum *de facto* drawn on the original agreement; it is inserted to rectify the count of the totals.

Agreement	Type	T	55	56	57	58	59	60	61	62	63	64	65	66	67	68	69	70	71	72	73	74	75	76	77	78	79	80	81	82	83	55–83
Agreement on development credits	*A	34	47																													26
	D																									26	Remainder	Transfered	to 1979	Agreement		26
	R	12	12																													26
	I	2½	2½								0.1	0.1	0.2	0.3	0.4	0.4	0.4	0.4	0.4	0.4	0.4	0.3	0.3	0.3	0.3	0.3						5.0
	LO						100C	100	100	100	99	96	91	86	81	76	74	74	74	74	74	74	74	74	74	74						
Protocol b'n Gov't of USSR and Prov'l Military Gov't of Ethiopia on econ'c and tech'l co-op'n	*A	34																							16							16
	D																											4	8	2		16
	R	12																													1	+
	I	2½																												0.3	0.3	0.3
	LO																														0	–
Protocol to econ'c and tech'l co-op'n (Revives and supplements 1959 credit)	*A	34																									149	149				149
	D																											15	20	38	40	113
	R	12																												3	5	8
	I	2½																										0.5	0.8	1.3	1.8	4.4
	LO																											149	134	114	76	36
Protocol to economic and technical co-operation (i)	*A	47																									31					31
	D																												8	6	6	20
	R	5+12																														
	I	2½																										0.1	0.2	0.2	0.3	0.5
	LO																											31	31	23	17	11
Protocol to economic and technical co-operation (ii)	*A	34																									15					15
	D																											7	8			15
	R	12																												1.2	1.2	2.4
	I	2½																										0.2	0.2	0.2	0.2	0.7
	LO																											15	8	0		
Protocol to econ'c and tech'l co-op'n / Agreement on construction of a cement works	*A	36																										77	77	77		77
	D	3+10																												8	15	23
	R																															
	I	3																													0.5	0.5
	LO																														69	54

Protocol		T	55	56	57	58	59	60	61	62	63	64	65	66	67	68	69	70	71	72	73	74	75	76	77	78	79	80	81	82	83	55-83
Protocol on economic and technical co-operation	A	100																											11	6		11
	D																												5			11
	R	-																														
	I	-																														
	LO																															
Protocol on economic and technical co-operation	A	100																											23	6		23
	D																												3	16	4	23
	R	-																														
	I	-																														
	LO																													20		
Protocol on econ'c and tech'l co-op'n in construction of 'Melkana Vakana' HEP	A	36																													4	0
	D																														77	77
	R	3 +10																														
	I	3																														
	LO																															77
Protocol on economic and technical co-operation	A	50																													43	43
	D																															
	R	5 +12																														
	I	2½																														
	LO																															43
T O T A L S	A						100C	100	100	1	3	5	5	5	5	2									16	26	195	77	34		120	468
	D																										2	26	52	76	65	247
	R														2.0	2.0	2.0	2.0	2.0	2.0	2.0	3.0	3.0	2.0	2.0	2.0			5.1	4.2	7.5	37.7
	I										0.1	0.1	0.2	0.3	0.4	0.4	0.4	0.4	0.4	0.4	0.4	0.3	0.3	0.3	0.3	0.3		0.6	1.0	1.7	3.1	11.4
	LO									100	99	96	91	86	81	76	74	74	74	74	74	74	74	74	74	90	16	209	260	242	166	221
Soviet Foreign Trade Statistics	D											2.2	6.1	2.9	7.0	0.6	0.3	...		0.2	0.4	0.5	0.4	0.2	0.2	1.9	2.2	5.1	13.6	16.5	25.7	66.0

GHANA

The Soviet Union and Ghana opened diplomatic relations in 1958. In 1959 talks were held on the construction of an iron and steel works, and in the following year a framework economic co-operation agreement was signed. It was aimed at geological prospecting, power stations, processing industries including an iron foundry, a fisheries combine, refrigeration equipment, and textiles. The credit was intended to cover feasibility studies in the first instance, but contained a considerable sum also towards project completion; one of the main projects considered was a dam and hydro-electric power station at Boui on the Volta. In 1961 a new co-operation agreement was signed covering such things as the production of reinforced concrete, engineering, the paper industry, technical schools, state farms, and nuclear research. The 1963 credit was for Soviet supplies of goods to be sold in Ghana to provide for some of the local Soviet costs.

The Boui dam was never completed, and judging by Soviet export statistics many of the other projects were not started, although funds could have been diverted to some extent for services.

In 1968 Soviet experts were in Accra to discuss further co-operation—pre-fabricated housing construction, fish canning, and a gold refinery, but no agreements were published. In 1982 the Ghanaian government expressed the wish to have the past credits re-activated, but instead a new credit was agreed of $10m. Since it was lent at 5% and was repayable in ten years it fell below 25% grant element and is therefore excluded here.

All agreements were published in the Soviet Treaty series except the third, which was well documented in Goldman's book.

Item		T	55	56	57	58	59	60	61	62	63	64	65	66	67	68	69	70	71	72	73	74	75	76	77	78	79	80	81	82	83	55–83
Agreement on economic and technical co-operation	A	34						40																								40
	D																															35
	R	12								2	6	6	8	6				3	2	2												35
	I	2½								0.1	0.3	0.4	0.4	0.4	0.4	0.4	0.4	0.5	0.5	0.5	0.5	0.5	0.5	0.5	0.5	0.4	0.4	0.4				8.0
	LO								40	38	32	26	18	12	12	12	12	9	7	5	5	5	5	5	5	5	5	5	5	5	5	5
Agreement on economic and technical co-operation	A	34							42																							42
	D																															23
	R	12										4	7	5	1			2	2	2												23
	I	2½																0.3	0.3	0.3	0.3	0.3	0.3	0.3	0.3	0.3	0.3	0.3	0.3			3.7
	LO									42	42	38	31	26	25	25	25	23	21	19	19	19	19	19	19	19	19	19	19	19	19	19
Development credit	*A	34																														22
	D													2																		6
	R	12												1	2				1	1	1											6.0
	I	2½																														1.0
	LO												22	21	19	19	19	19	18	17	16	16	16	16	16	16	16	16	16	16	16	16
TOTALS	A							40																								104
	D								2	6	10	15	12	3			5	5	5	1												64
	R											0.4	0.4	0.4	0.4	0.4	2.0	3.0	5.0	5.5	5.5	5.5	5.5	5.5	5.5	5.5	5.5	5.5	2.5	0.5	0.5	64.0
	I									0.1	0.3	0.4	1.0	0.4	0.4	0.4	0.4	0.9	0.9	0.9	0.9	0.9	0.9	0.9	0.9	0.8	0.7	0.8	0.3	0.1		12.7
	LO								40	80	74	86	71	59	56	56	56	51	46	41	40	40	40	40	40	40	40	40	40	40	40	40
Soviet Foreign Trade Statictics	D								0.1	2.6	4.6	4.4	8.1	0.7			3.3	2.7														26.5

GRENADA

In February 1981 Grenada Radio announced deliveries from the Soviet Union of equipment for the agricultural sector—irrigation pumps, bulldozers, trucks, tractors, and spare parts, referring to an (unpublished) agreement of the previous year. In July the two agreements included in the tables were signed in Moscow. The commodity credit was to cover some of the Soviet local co-operation costs; the second, apart from a satellite tracking station, was to look at the economic and technical prospects of an east coast port and improved water supplies and sewage disposal.

Both agreements were announced by TASS on 27 July 1982 and St Georges' Domestic Service on 29 July 1982.

		T	55	56	57	58	59	60	61	62	63	64	65	66	67	68	69	70	71	72	73	74	75	76	77	78	79	80	81	82	83	55-83
Commodity credit	*A	100																												1.5		1.5
	D																													0.2	1.0	1.2
	R																															
	I																															
	LO																															
Feasibility studies and satellite station	*A	36																													1.3	0.3
	D																													7.5		7.5
	R	3 +10																													3	3
	I	3																														
	LO																															
T O T A L S	A																														7.5	4.5
	D																													9		9
	R																													0.2	4.0	4.2
	I																															
	LO																														8.8	4.8

GUINEA

The first trade agreement between the Soviet Union and Guinea was concluded in February 1959, and the first economic co-operation agreement six months later. The credit was on the standard terms of $2\frac{1}{2}\%$ with twelve years repayment; it was designed partly for feasibility studies for such projects as a dam on the river Fia and bauxite development, and partly for the construction of smaller projects such as cold storage, a hotel and sports stadium in Conakry, a cannery at Mamou, a sawmill at N'Zerekore, and a radio station. Reference is made in later agreements to other credits in 1960 and 1962 which, with the fisheries credit, was claimed to bring the total by the end of 1966 up to $73m, but the other agreements were not published and may have had some military connections. In September a new framework credit was agreed, suggesting that the previous credits were becoming exhausted.

In November 1969 the Soviet Union and Guinea signed a major agreement for the comprehensive development and exploitation of the Kindia bauxite deposit. This included not only prospecting, surveying, and mining but also the development of roads, railways, and port facilities; it was to be repaid by Soviet purchases of bauxite. Soviet investment in the bauxite industry was further increased by part of the 1973 credit, but this was also destined for the construction of a 10 MW hydro-electric power station.

It was typical of many of these co-operation agreements that they included a large element of credit for Soviet goods to be sold in Guinea to help meet local costs.

All agreements were published in the Soviet Treaty series.

		T	55	56	57	58	59	60	61	62	63	64	65	66	67	68	69	70	71	72	73	74	75	76	77	78	79	80	81	82	83	55-83
Agreement on economic and technical co-operation	A	34					35						4	1	3	3	3	4	4	4	4	2	2	1								35
	D																															35
	R	12						3	7	7	7	6	2	2	0.5	0.5	0.5	0.5	0.5	0.5	0.5	0.5	0.3	0.3								35
	I	2½								0.1	0.1	0.2	0.5	0.5	0.5	0.5	0.5	0.5	0.5	0.5	0.5	0.5	0.3	0.3								6.0
	LO							35	32	25	18	11	5	1	0																	
Protocol to Agreement on co-operation in the fisheries industry	A	34												4	2	2												0.4				4
	D																															4
	R	12																	0.3	0.3	0.3	0.3	0.3	0.3	0.4	0.4	0.4	0.4	0.3	0.3	0.3	4.0
	I	2½																	0.1	0.1	0.1	0.1	0.1	0.1	0.1	0.1	0.1					0.6
	LO														4	2	0											0.4				
Agreement on extending economic and technical co-operation	A	34													17																	17
	D																5	5	3													17
	R	12																	0.5	1.5	1.5	1.5	1.5	1.5	1.5	1.5	1.5	1.5	1.5	1.5	1.5	17.0
	I	2½																0.1	0.2	0.3	0.3	0.3	0.3	0.3	0.2	0.2	0.2	0.2	0.2	0.2	0.2	3.2
	LO															17	14	9	4	1	0											
Agree't on co-op'n in the formation and exploitation of a national bauxite industry	A	34															92	92	4	38	45	3	2			7	8	8	8	8		92
	D																															92
	R	12																								7	7	8	8	8	8	8	68
	I	2½																			0.4		1.3	1.3	1.3	1.3	1.3	1.2	1.2	1.2	1.2	13.0
	LO																92	92	92	88	50	5	2	0								
Agreement on questions of economic and technical co-operation	A	34																				32					4	4	2	2	3	3	32
	D																						4	8	16	2	2	2	2	3	3	32
	R	12																															14
	I	2½																						0.2	0.5	0.5	0.5	0.5	0.4	0.4	0.4	3.5
	LO																					32	28	24	16	10	6	2	0			

	T	55	56	57	58	59	60	61	62	63	64	65	66	67	68	69	70	71	72	73	74	75	76	77	78	79	80	81	82	83	55-83
A						35								17		92				32											180
D							3	7	7	7	6	4	4	2	5	5	5	7	39	45	7	6	8	6	4	4	2				180
R									0.1	0.1	1.0	2.0	2.0	3.0	3.0	3.3	4.3	4.8	5.8	5.8	3.8	10.8	9.8	8.9	10.9	11.9	11.9	11.5	12.5	11.0	138.0
I											0.2	0.5	0.5	0.5	0.5	0.6	0.7	0.8	0.8	1.2	2.1	1.9	2.0	2.0	2.0	2.0	1.9	1.9	1.8	1.6	25.7
LO							35	32	25	18	11	5	1	4	19	14	101	96	89	50	37	30	24	16	10	6	2	0			
TOTALS																															
Soviet Foreign Trade Statistics — D								0.1	9.1	7.4	7.4	3.9	1.9	3.4	1.0	1.9			36.6	38.1	7.7	9.7	5.4	5.0	7.1	8.4	8.0	20.2	14.5	15.4	212.2

GUINEA-BISSAU

The President of Guinea-Bissau visited Moscow early in 1975, and signed an agreement with Kosygin on closer co-operation in economic, scientific, and cultural co-operation. The first economic protocol was signed in 1976; it envisaged co-operation in prospecting for bauxite, and included equipment for a geological laboratory and the provision of Soviet goods to help cover local costs. The new, larger protocol signed in 1982 was on stiffer terms; it extended the 1975 and 1976 agreements to 1986, and was intended for drilling for water, electrification, and construction materials.

Both agreements were published in the Soviet Treaty series.

Agreement		T	55	56	57	58	59	60	61	62	63	64	65	66	67	68	69	70	71	72	73	74	75	76	77	78	79	80	81	82	83	55-83
Protocol to Agreement on econ'c and tech'l co-operation of 21 Feb 1975	A	63																						2.9								2.9
	D																								0.9	1.0	1.0					2.9
	R	5 +12																										0.1			0.2	0.2
	I	-																										0.0		0.1		0.2
	LO																								2.9	2.0	1.0					
Protocol to Agreement on econ'c and tech'l co-operation of 21 Feb 1975	A	25																												6.9		6.9
	D																														2.9	2.9
	R	10																														
	I	4																														
	LO																															4.0
T O T A L S	A																							2.9						6.9		9.8
	D																								0.9	1.0	1.0				2.9	5.8
	R																											0.1			0.2	0.2
	I																											0.0		0.1		0.2
	LO																								2.9	2.0	1.0					4.0

INDIA

The story of Soviet economic co-operation with India is long and extensive. India launched her first Five year Economic Development Plan in 1951 with the emphasis on state-owned industries, and soon after the Soviet Union began talks on the construction of an integrated iron and steel works at Bhilai, in Madhya Pradesh. The first Indo-Soviet co-operation agreement, signed in 1955, centred on this plant, whose first stage was completed in 1961 and second stage in 1968.

In 1957 the Soviet Union agreed to open a general credit to cover a range of projects under India's second Five Year Plan, and since then there have been regular agreements on credits either for specific projects or for India's Five Year Plans. The list of major Soviet-assisted projects constructed, or under construction, in India includes the Bhilai, Bokaro, and Visakhapatnam iron and steel works; a heavy engineering plant at Ranchi with its subsidiary mining machinery plant at Durgapur; oil refineries at Gujarat, Barauni, Koyali, and Mathura; the Bharat heavy electrical plant at Hardwar; an aluminium plant at Korba and other non-ferrous projects; deep and open-cast coalmining, thermal and hydro-electric power plants, pharmaceutical works, and oil and gas prospecting.

One provision which has very much facilitated this co-operation has been the central rouble–rupee accounting system covering over 99% of all transactions between the two countries, thus excluding any reference to convertible currency. Another great advantage to India has been the willingness and ability of the Soviet Union to accept in repayment goods such as railway equipment which were surplus to Indian requirements while the domestic market was being built up, and which may not have had a very strong export potential elsewhere.

The 1977 credit (250m roubles) was offered to the short-lived Jenata party government. It was intended for the iron and steel industry and coalmining at Singrauli and Raniganj, but implementation may have been delayed by negotiations over the rouble–rupee exchange rate, which at 1:8 very much favoured the Indian side. When the Congress I returned to power the rate was changed to 1:10 in November 1978, and the 250m roubles was again agreed, but directed more specifically to the Visakhapatnam iron and steel works.

All the agreements except the first two were published in the Soviet Treaty series; the first two were widely documented, including the Indian Ministry of Finance publication *External Assistance*, 1959, pp. 16 and 17.

		T	55	56	57	58	59	60	61	62	63	64	65	66	67	68	69	70	71	72	73	74	75	76	77	78	79	80	81	82	83	55-83
Bhilai Iron and Steel Plant	+A	34	136						117																							253
	D			4	25	30	40	30	7		17	20	30	30	15	5																253
	R	12								12	12	12	19	22	22	22	22	22														253
	I	2½		0.5	1.0	1.0	1.5	2.0	2.0	2.0	1.5	2.0	3.4	3.6	3.6	3.6	3.6	3.6		1.6	1.6	1.6	1.6	1.6								43.0
	LO		136	132	107	77	37	7	117	117	100	80	50	20	5	0																	
General credit Second Five Year Plan	+A	34			125																											125
	D					10	20	50	18																							98
	R	12											5	4	8	8	8	8	8	8	8											98
	I	2½								1.7	1.7	1.7	1.7	1.7	1.7	1.7	1.7	1.7	1.7	1.7	1.7	1.7	1.7	1.7								22.0
	LO				125	115	95	45	27	27	27	27	27	27	27	27	27	27	27	27	27	27	27	27	27	27	27	27	27	27	27	27
Agreement on co-operation in construction of plants for medical products	A	25					20																										20
	D									2	7	5	3	3	3	3	3	3														20
	R	7											5	2	3	3	3	3														20
	I	2½								0.1	0.2	0.3	0.3	0.3	0.3	0.3	0.3	0.2														2.3
	LO							20	20	19	17	10	5	2	0																	
Agreement on extension of a credit for co-op'n in realization of Third FYP	+A	34					125	250																								375
	D							6	30	60	90	90	45	40	10	4																375
	R	12											33	33	33	33	33	33	33	33	33	33	33									375
	I	2½										5.1	5.1	5.1	5.1	5.1	5.1	5.1	5.1	4.8	4.8	4.8	4.8									66.0
	LO							369	339	279	189	99	54	14	4	0																	
Supplementary credit for Third Five Year Plan	+A	34							125																							125
	D									2	2	10	20	30	30	15	10	5	3													125
	R	12													11	11	11	11	11	11	11	11	11	11	11	11						125
	I	2½												1.7	1.7	1.7	1.7	1.7	1.7	1.7	1.7	1.7	1.7	1.7	1.7	1.7	0.9					23.0
	LO									125	123	113	93	63	33	18	8	3	0														
Agree't on co-op'n in constr'n of an iron and steel plant in Bokaro & ext'n of a credit	A	34											211																			211
	D													11					40	60	80	15	20									211
	R	12																						20	20	20	20	20	20	20	20	201
	I	2½																	1.0	2.0	3.0	2.9	2.9	2.9	2.9	2.9	2.9	2.9	2.9	2.9	2.9	35.0
	LO												211	211	211	211	211	211	200	160	100	20	0									

Agreement		T	55	56	57	58	59	60	61	62	63	64	65	66	67	68	69	70	71	72	73	74	75	76	77	78	79	80	81	82	83	55‑83
Agree't on econ'c and tech'l co‑op'n in construction of industrial and other projects	A	34												333																		333
	D															3	5	10	15	20	30	30	30	30	15	15	10	10	10	10	10	253
	R	12																				5	5	5	5	5	5	10	10	20	20	90
	I	2½																				1	1	1	1	1	1	2	2	2	3	15
	LO														333	333	330	325	315	300	280	250	220	190	160	145	130	120	110	100	90	80
Agreement on economic and technical co‑operation	A	47																						375				Agreement				
	D																											transferred				
	R	3 +17																										to				
	I	2½																										Agreement				
	LO																										of 1979					
Agree't on co‑op'n in the construct'n of the 1st stage of Visakhapatnam Iron & Steel Works	A	47																								383					383
	D																													50	120	170
	R	3 +17																														
	I	2½																														
	LO																										383	383	383	333	213
Agreement on economic and technical co‑operation	A	47																									800				800
	D																													6	10	16
	R	3 +17																														
	I	2½																														
	LO																										800	800	800	794	784
Agree't on co‑op'n in the construct'n of the 2nd stage of Visakhapatnam Iron & Steel Works	A	47																												189	189
	D																															
	R	3 +17																														
	I	2½																														
	LO																													189	189

	T	55	56	57	58	59	60	61	62	63	64	65	66	67	68	69	70	71	72	73	74	75	76	77	78	79	80	81	82	83	55-83
T O T A L S	A	136		125		145	250	242				211	333													383	800			189	2814
	D		4	25	40	60	86	56	64	124	135	108	102	40	22	10	24	55	80	110	50	30	30	15	15	10	10	10	66	140	1521
	R					4	12	12	18	18	34	63	70	77	77	77	77	62	62	68	77	82	46	36	25	25	30	30	40	40	1162
	I			0.5	1.0	1.0	2.0	4.0	5.6	6.7	9.1	10.5	12.4	12.4	12.4	12.4	12.3	11.1	11.8	12.8	12.3	12.2	7.2	5.6	5.6	4.8	4.9	4.9	4.9	5.9	206.3
	LO	136	136	132	232	192	277	441	627	563	439	304	407	638	598	576	566	542	487	407	297	247	217	187	172	157	530	1320	1310	1244	1293
Soviet Foreign Trade Statistics	D	0.1	5.8	43.3	98.1	34.2	18.1	39.6	64.7	81.3	133	101	64.3	90.4	113	102	69.3		48.7	55.3	71.5	82.4	94.4	86.3	59.6	50.4	119	92.9	90.4	129	2037

INDONESIA

The first period of Soviet economic co-operation with Indonesia started in 1956 with a large general credit on slightly better than the standard Soviet terms at that time; it was intended for feasibility studies and construction in mining, non-ferrous metals, hydro-electric power, construction, a steelworks at Tjigela, a superphosphate plant, a slphur works, two mechanized rice farms, road construction, and nuclear research.

After the fall of Sukarno there was a hiatus in Soviet–Indonesian economic co-operation. This was ended by an agreement signed in 1970 for the rescheduling of Indonesian debts, a new co-operation agreement in 1974, and a soviet credit for the construction of an aluminium plant on Bintan island in 1976; the terms, however, took these just outside the 'aid' category.

In the tables the repayment and interest payments are purely theoretical. The 1970 agreement suggests that Indonesia would have defaulted at some stage on its debts, but the sum owing, quoted as very nearly $800m, must have included other debts such as short-term and military debts, and it is not possible to separate them with the information available. The theoretical repayments are shown for the purpose of consistency.

The first three agreements were well documented at the time, and were included in Goldman and Müller. The fourth agreement and the debt rescheduling were included in the Soviet Treaty series.

Item	Code	Terms	55	56	57	58	59	60	61	62	63	64	65	66	67	68	69	70	71	72	73	74	75	76	77	78	79	80	81	82	83	55-83
General project credit – I	*A	T 41		100																												100
	D					10	25	25	25	10	5																					100
	R	3 +12										8	8	8	8	8	8	8	8	8	8	8	6	4	2							100
	I	2½						1	1	1	1	1	1	1	1	1	1	1	1	1	1	1	1	1	1							18
	LO				100	100	90	65	40	15	5	0																				
Oceanographic Research Institute	*A	41					5																									5
	D							2	3																							5
	R	3 +12										0.4	0.4	0.4	0.4	0.4	0.4	0.4	0.4	0.4	0.4	0.5	0.5									5.0
	I	2½										0.1	0.1	0.1	0.1	0.1	0.1	0.1	0.1	0.1	0.1											1.0
	LO																															
Asian Games complex	*A	41					12																									12
	D							2	7	3																						12
	R	3 +12										1	1	1	1	1	1	1	1	1	1	1	1									12.0
	I	2½							0.1	0.1	0.1	0.1	0.1	0.1	0.1	0.1	0.1	0.1	0.1	0.1	0.1											1.3
	LO							12	10	3	0																					
2nd General Agreement on economic and technical co-operation	A	34						250																								250
	D								12	15	30	40	40	3																		140
	R	12											11	11	11	11	12	12	12	12	12	12	12	12								140
	I	2½									1	2	2	3	2	2	2	2	2	2	2	2	2	1								26
	LO							250	250	238	223	193	153	113	110	110	110	110	110	110	110	110	110	110	110	110	110	110	110	110	110	110
TOTALS	A			100			17	250																								367
	D					10	25	29	47	28	35	40	40	3																		257
	R											9.4	20.4	20.4	20.4	20.4	21.4	21.4	21.4	21.4	21.4	21.5	19.5	16.0	2.0							257.0
	I							1.0	1.1	1.2	2.2	3.2	3.2	3.2	3.2	3.2	3.1	3.2	3.1	3.1	3.1	3.1	3.1	2.0	1.0							46.3
	LO				100	100	90	82	303	256	228	193	153	113	110	110	110	110	110	110	110	110	110	110	110	110	110	110	110	110	110	110
Soviet Foreign Trade Statistics	D							5.0	9.0	7.4	9.7	18.5	13.2	3.8	0.3																	66.9

IRAN

Soviet economic co-operation with Iran began in July 1963 with an agreement for the construction of a hydro-electric project at Tabriz, a fish processing factory, and eleven silos with a total capacity of 80,000 tonnes of grain. Repayments were scheduled over twelve years, but the interest rate, at 3.6%, was higher than the Soviet practice at that time.

In January 1966, in the aftermath of Shah Pahlavi's visit to the USSR the previous June, a wide-ranging new agreement was signed with a 260m rouble credit for the construction of a steel mill near Isfahan, a heavy engineering plant near Arak, and a large-diameter gas pipeline; the terms were improved to the Soviet standard of $2\frac{1}{2}$%. In 1967 it was reported that the Soviet Union had agreed to give credits for the construction of 22 new silos under a 20 rouble credit, repayable in eight years at $2\frac{1}{2}$%.

Under a new agreement in June 1968 the Soviet Union extended a credit of 160m roubles to help finance Iran's fourth Five Year Plan (March 1968 to March 1973). Among the projects mentioned were the Aryamehr steel mill near Isfahan, a lead and zinc plant, and a 140km electrified railway from Tabriz to the border town of Dzhulfa. By March 1973 the first stage of the steelworks was completed, and the Russians offered a new loan of 140m roubles for its expansion.

In December 1976 the two sides were talking of extending their economic co-operation, including the further expansion of Aryamehr from the planned 1.9m tonnes to 6lm tonnes; the heavy engineering plant at Arak was also to be enlarged. Political factors, however, interrupted these operations and economic co-operation was not resumed until mid-1980.

By the end of 1983 the following projects had been completed with Soviet assistance: the Aryamehr iron and steel works up to an annual capacity of 1.9m tonnes of steel, the heavy engineering plant at Arak up to a capacity of 25,000 tones of machinery, a thermal power station at Ahwaz (1,260 MW), 41 silos with a total capacity of 900,000 tonnes of grain, and 23 scientific and technical training centres. A 1000km pipeline to the Soviet border to carry associated gas to the energy-deficient trans-Caucasus was more than half built by the Russians; and in 1978 an agreement was signed, and construction started, for a large-diameter pipeline to boost Soviet sales of natural gas to Western Europe, but the project was abandoned in 1982. It is not known exactly

Agreement		T	55	56	57	58	59	60	61	62	63	64	65	66	67	68	69	70	71	72	73	74	75	76	77	78	79	80	81	82	83	55-83
Agreement on economic and technical co-operation	A	29									39																					39
	D											1	1	3	10	15	7	2														39
	R																3	3	3	3	3	3	3	3	3	4	4	4				39
	I																0.8	0.8	0.8	0.8	0.8	0.8	0.7	0.7	0.7	0.7	0.7	0.7				9.0
	LO											38	37	34	24	9	2	0														
Agree't on co-op'n in the constr'n of indust'l and other projects and ext'n of a credit	A	34												289																		289
	D														4	20	100	80	60	20	5											289
	R	12																	24	24	24	24	24	24	24	24	24	24	24	24	25	289
	I	2½																														47
	LO														285	265	165	85	25	5	0											
Agreement on additional silos	+A	27													22																	22
	D																3	3	3	3	3	3	2	2								22
	R	8																					1	2	2	2	2	2	2	2	3	18
	I	2½																				0.3	0.3	0.3	0.3	0.3	0.3	0.3	0.3	0.3	0.3	3.0
	LO															22	19	16	13	10	7	4	2	0								
Agreement on economic and technical co-operation	A	27														178																178
	D																8	20	70	50	20	10										178
	R	8																					22	22	22	22	22	22	23	23		178
	I	2½																														19.2
	LO															178	170	150	80	30	10	0										
Agreement in the sphere of production/technical teaching	A	34																10														10
	D																			5	5											10
	R	12																				1	1	1	1	1	1	1	1	1	1	10
	I	2½																				0.2	0.2	0.2	0.2	0.1	0.1	0.1	0.1	0.1	0.1	1.6
	LO																	10	10	5	0											
Agree't on co-op'n in enlarging iron and steel plant 'Aryamehr' in Isfahan	A	34																			188											188
	D																					8	70	70	30	10						188
	R	12																								15	15	15	15	16	16	92
	I	2½																								3	3	3	3	3	3	18
	LO																				188	180	110	40	10	0						

what was the concessionality of these agreements; it is only known that repayment and interest were to be met by gas deliveries.

All the co-operation agreements with Iran were published in the Soviet Treaty series except the third, which was published in *BfA/NfA* (A) of 13 October 1972, and was later confirmed by the announcement of the total number of grain silos built with Soviet assistance.

	T	55	56	57	58	59	60	61	62	63	64	65	66	67	68	69	70	71	72	73	74	75	76	77	78	79	80	81	82	83	55-83
TOTALS A										39			289	22	178	118	10	138	78	188	20	72	70	30	10						726
D																	105			28											726
R											1	1	3	14	38	3	3	3	27	28	51	51	52	52	68	68	69	65	42	44	626
I																0.8	0.8	0.8	4.8	5.0	7.7	7.6	7.6	7.6	10.5	10.5	10.5	9.8	7.4	6.4	97.8
LO											39	38	37	323	331	471	353	258	120	42	202	182	110	40	10	0					
Soviet Foreign Trade Statistics D						0.2							4.8	22.4	36.7	109	127		40.6	97.5	149	168	135	136	172	161	112	153	114	171	1909

IRAQ

The first economic co-operation agreement between the Soviet Union and Iraq was signed in March 1959. Among the 35 projects included were a steel mill near Baghdad, a nitric fertilizer plant at Basra, and a sulphur plant; plants for the manufacture of agricultural machinery and equipment, electrical equipment, glass, light bulbs, pharmaceuticals, cotton and wool textiles, knitwear and clothing; and railways, a radio station, granaries, canneries, and state farms. The credit for 500 old roubles was at the standard rate of $2\frac{1}{2}\%$ with twelve years to repay. In August 1960 an additional credit of 180m old roubles on the same terms was mainly intended for the 550km Baghdad–Basra railway.

The projects completed by the end of 1968 included the railway, an electrical equipment factory, a clothing factory, a nuclear reactor in Baghdad, a radio station, a cannery, and several agricultural undertakings. The total number of projects had been reduced to 22, but it is assumed that the favourable credits would nevertheless have been taken up in full.

In July 1969 the two sides agreed to co-operate in the major project of the development of the North Rumeilah oilfield. The 1969 and 1971 credits totalled 75m new roubles, and a proportion of the 1975 and 1976 credits were allocated to this project. Although the interest rate remained at $2\frac{1}{2}\%$, the repayment period was reduced to seven years. A massive 200m rouble credit for an oil refinery at Mosul, a 540km pipeline from Basra to Baghdad, and several other major projects was repayable in six years and therefore its concessionality falls below 25% grant element. By April 1974 the first two stages of the North Rumeilah oilfield development were operating with a total capacity of 23m tonnes of crude per annum, and the third stage, raising the capacity to 42m tonnes, was completed in 1975. At the same time the North Rumeilah pipeline to Basra was extended south-west to the oil export terminal at Fao. The Soviet Union was also very much involved in the development of the Ruheis deposit, and by the end of 1983 had become closely concerned in the development of the West Qurnah field.

The Soviet Union has been involved in a great many major and minor projects in Iraq apart from those in the oil industry. Among the most important there are a series of dams, hydro-electric power stations and irrigation schemes on the Euphrates, the Euphrates–Tharthar canal, the Basra iron and steel plant, the fisheries and textile industries, electrical equipment, mineral prospecting, pharmaceuticals, phos-

	T	55	56	57	58	59	60	61	62	63	64	65	66	67	68	69	70	71	72	73	74	75	76	77	78	79	80	81	82	83	55–83
Agreement on economic and technical co-operation — A	34					138																									138
D																															138
R	12																														138
I	2½																														24.0
LO							138	135	125	85	45	25	15	10																	
Agreement on economic and technical co-operation — A	34						45																								45
D	12							10	40	40	20	10	5	4	3	3															45
R									4	6	6	6	6	6	12	12	12	12	12	12	12	12	7	4	3	3					45
I	2½										2	2	2	2	2	2	2	2	2	2	2	2		1							8
LO								45	43	39	33	27	21	15	9	4	0														
Agreement on econ'c and tech'l co-op'n to develop Iraqi oil prod'n industry — A	25															67															67
D	7																4	4	5	8	10	15	10	10	10	10	10	10	10	4	67
R																															67
I	2½																			0.9	0.9	0.9	0.9	0.9	0.9	0.9	0.9	0.9	0.9	0.9	7.2
LO																	67	63	59	54	46	36	21	11	5	0					
Protocol to Agreement of 4th July 1969 — A	25																														18
D																				2	3	5	5	3	3	3	2	2	2	2	18
R																								2	3	3	2	2	2		18
I	2½																				0.1	0.2	0.3	0.3	0.3	0.2	0.2	0.2	0.2		2.0
LO																			18	18	16	13	8	3	0						
Agreement on economic and technical co-operation — A	25																						158	4	15	50	80	80	70	30	337
D																								8	15	50	80	80	70	30	337
R	7																												20	5	50
I	2½																												5	5	10
LO																							179	333	325	310	260	180	100	30	0

phates, cement, electrification, water supplies, road construction, and many aspects of agriculture including large grain silos.

All Soviet–Iraq economic co-operation agreements were published in the Soviet Treaty series.

	T	55	56	57	58	59	60	61	62	63	64	65	66	67	68	69	70	71	72	73	74	75	76	77	78	79	80	81	82	83	55-83
T O T A L S A						138	45									67			18			179	158								605
D							3	12	44	46	26	16	11	10	8	7	4	4	5	10	13	20	19	17	20	50	80	80	70	30	605
R											6	8	10	11	15	16	16	16	16	16	16	16	16	16	16	16	12	12	32	36	318
I											2.0	2.0	3.0	2.0	3.0	3.0	3.0	3.0	2.0	3.0	2.1	3.2	1.2	2.2	1.2	1.1	1.1	1.1	6.1	5.9	51.2
LO							138	180	168	124	78	52	36	25	15	7	67	63	59	72	62	49	208	347	330	310	260	180	100	30	0
Soviet Foreign Trade Statistics D						0.2	4.3	15.9	29.7	25.9	18.0	5.4	4.3	4.6	4.7	2.3	3.9		23.3	44.9	50.3	64.8	105	163	211	269	159	87.3	73.4	59.8	1430

JORDAN

A Soviet economic delegation visited Jordan in January 1968 and twelve months later an economic co-operation agreement was signed. A protocol to this agreement gave the terms and values of a credit to be used for geological prospecting and the construction of technical schools; part of the credit was to be used for the import of Soviet goods for sale to help defray local expenses. An exchange of letters in June 1976 offered a large new credit on the same terms; this was to be used for technical schools, but was also available for rural electrification and as a contribution towards the expenses of Jordanians studying in the Soviet Union.

The agreement and the exchange of letters were published in the Soviet Treaty series.

	T	55	56	57	58	59	60	61	62	63	64	65	66	67	68	69	70	71	72	73	74	75	76	77	78	79	80	81	82	83	55-83
A	34															5.5							20							1.0	25.5
D																					0.5	1.0	1.0	2.0	2.0	3.0	3.0	3.0	2.0	1.0	18.5
R	12																								1	1	1	1	2	3	8
I	24																									0.2	0.2	0.2	0.2	0.2	1.0
LO																	5.5	5.5	5.5	5.5	5.5	5.0	4.0	23.0	21.0	19.0	16.0	13.0	10.0	8.0	7.0

Protocol to Agreement on economic and technical co-operation

KAMPUCHEA

Official Soviet–Kampuchean economic relations opened with a payments agreement in 1957. In 1960 the Russians offered Kampuchea the gift of equipment for a hospital, and in the following year of a higher educational establishment. The first economic co-operation agreement was signed in April 1963; it was on the standard contemporary Soviet terms of $2\frac{1}{2}\%$ interest with twelve years to repay, and was offered for the construction of a dam, hydro-electric power station, and high tension lines on the river Kamchai.

There was some Soviet military aid announced in 1968 to a value of $6m, but apparently no further economic assistance until the start of a series of commodity grants and two development credits in 1979.

The largest single Soviet operation in Kampuchea has been the establishment of a construction organization under the 1981 credit. This national organization would have been helpful for the ultilization of the other development credits.

The first and last three agreements were contained in the Soviet Treaty series; the 1979 and 1980 commodity grants and development credits were announced by the Soviet representative to the United Nations (UN reference A/35/763 of 12 December 1980), and all four commodity grants by a Soviet spokesman in Phnom Penh quoted by AFP on 3 February 1983.

Description		T	55	56	57	58	59	60	61	62	63	64	65	66	67	68	69	70	71	72	73	74	75	76	77	78	79	80	81	82	83	55-83
Protocol on ext'n of economic and tech'l co-op'n in constr'n of an HEP on the r. Kamchai	A	34									12																					12
	D															1	1	1	1	1	1	1	1	1	1	1						12
	R	12										3	5	4																		12
	I	24													0	0.2	0.2	0.2	0.2	0.2	0.2	0.2	0.1	0.1	0.1	0.1						2.0
	LO											12	9	4	0																	
Commodity relief aid	+A	100																									85	134	95	15		329
	D	–																									85	134	95	15	20	329
	R	–																														
	I																															
	LO																															
Development	+A	34																										70	80			150
	D																											10	30	70	20	130
	R	12																														
	I	24																														
	LO																															
Credits	A	57																											60	110	40	20
	D																															
	R	20																											1	2	2	5
	I																															
	LO																															
Agreement on offer of co-operation in founding a State construction organization	A	72																											56			56
	D																												5	35	16	56
	R	5 +20																													8	8
	I																															
	LO																															
Agr't on ext'n of econ'c and tech'l co-operation in construction of projects (i)	A	100																												51	16	0
	D																													38	8	38
	R	–																													38	30
	I																															
	LO																															
Agr't on ext'n of econ'c and tech'l co-operation in construction of projects (ii)	A	100																												11	11	11
	D																														5	5
	R	–																													5	
	I																															
	LO																														11	6

	T	55	56	57	58	59	60	61	62	63	64	65	66	67	68	69	70	71	72	73	74	75	76	77	78	79	80	81	82	83	55-83
T O T A L S A										12																85	204	231	64		596
D											3	5	4													85	144	130	120	49	540
R																															12
I														1	1	1	1	1	1	1	1	1	1	1	1			1	2	2	2.0
														0.2	0.2	0.2	0.2	0.2	0.2	0.2	0.2	0.1	0.1	0.1	0.1						
LO											12	9	4	0														60	161	105	56
Soviet Foreign Trade Statistics D											0.6	0.2	0.2																		1.0

KENYA

None of the projects envisaged under the 1964 co-operation agreement reached fruition, although some expenditure is shown in the table and is likely to have been made for Soviet technical assistance, including doctors. The second credit was to provide equipment for a hospital at Kisumu, with the Kenyans responsible for the construction. This project was successfully completed.

The first agreement was in the Soviet Treaty series; the agreement on Kisumu hospital was reported in *Blick durch die Wirtschaft* on 5 January 1972 and confirmed by the Soviet economic representatives in Nairobi.

		T	55	56	57	58	59	60	61	62	63	64	65	66	67	68	69	70	71	72	73	74	75	76	77	78	79	80	81	82	83	55-83
Agreement on ec. and tech'l co-op'n in constr'n of industrial and agric'l projects	A	41										44																				.44
	D																															12
	R	3 +12														0.1			0.1		0.1		0.1	0.2	0.2	0.2	0.2	0.4	0.4	0.4	0.6	3.0
	I	2½																									0.1	0.2	0.2	0.2	0.2	1.0
	LO	2½											44	44	43	42	41	40	40	40	40	40	40	40	39	38	37	36	35	34	33	32
Kisumu Hospital	+A	34																														0.3
	D																			0.3	0.3									0.1		0.3
	R	12																				0.1				0.1					0.1		0.3
	I	2½																			0.3	0.0										...
	LO	2½																														
T O T A L S	A											44								0.3												44.3
	D																				0.3										1	12.3
	R														1	0.1	1		0.1		0.1		0.1	0.2	0.2	0.3	0.2	0.4	0.4	0.5	0.6	3.3
	I																										0.1	0.2	0.2	0.2	0.2	1.0
	LO												44	44	43	42	41	40	40	40	40.3	40	40	40	39	38	37	36	35	34	33	32

NORTH KOREA

Soviet economic assistance to North Korea started with a 1,000m old rouble grant in 1953 for the reconstruction of war-damaged projects, in particular the hydro-electric projects along the Yalu river. The agreement covered technical advisers and consumer goods—presumably to defray local costs—and also postponed or cancelled the repayment of previous debts, which may have been trade debts and which may have been military. The 1957 agreement was to recharge the previous credts, now reportedly almost exhausted, and contained clauses for further debt rescheduling or cancellation, as did the new agreement of 1966 for general industrial development.

The 1966 agreement was published in the Soviet Treaty series; the other agreements were reported in Goldman. Soviet trade statistics suggest low drawings between 1958 and 1961, but there is plenty of collateral information to suggest that the North Koreans normally took up their credits in full. The Soviet statistics after 1969 suggest drawings on unpublished agreements; these are unlikely to have been on 'aid' terms.

Note D: Includes previous years.

		T	55	56	57	58	59	60	61	62	63	64	65	66	67	68	69	70	71	72	73	74	75	76	77	78	79	80	81	82	83	55-83
Development grants	*A	100																														325
	D	2500D	2000	25	75	2	1	1	6	15	15	15	20																			325
	R	-																														-
(D = includes	I	-																														-
previous years)	LO			50	25	75	73	72	71	65	50	35	20	0																		
Agreement on ec.	A	46												178																		178
and tech'l co-op'n	D													15	50	70	30	13														178
in construct'n and	R	3 +14																	12.7	12.7	12.7	12.7	12.7	12.7	12.7	12.7	12.7	12.7	12.7	12.7	12.6	165.0
ext'n of indust'l	I	2													1.0	1.2	1.4	1.6	1.9	1.9	1.9	1.9	1.9	1.9	2.0	1.9	1.9	1.9	1.9	1.9	1.9	30.0
and other projects	LO														163	113	43	13	0													
	A	2500	2500		75									178																		503
	D	2000	2000	25	25	2	1	1	6	15	15	15	20	15	50	70	30	13														503
T O T A L S	R																		12.7	12.7	12.7	12.7	12.7	12.7	12.7	12.7	12.7	12.7	12.7	12.7	12.6	165.0
	I														1.0	1.2	1.4	1.6	1.9	1.9	1.9	1.9	1.9	1.9	2.0	1.9	1.9	1.9	1.9	1.9	1.9	30.0
	LO			50	25	75	73	72	71	65	50	35	20	0	163	113	43	13	0													
Soviet Foreign Trade Statistics	D		1.7	4.3	6.6	2.8	2.3	0.9	1.2	9.8	13.7	18.7	13.1	17.6	3.1	16.8	30.1	73.8		82.0	71.4	67.8	60.3	35.1	16.5	14.7	30.9	74.7	64.6	70.9	25.6	831.0

LAOS

The first trade and payments agreements between the USSR and Laos were signed in Moscow on 1 December 1962. On the same date the Russians agreed to extend a credit of 3.5m roubles on their standard terms ($2\frac{1}{2}$% with twelve years to repay) for the construction of a hydro-electric power station, and promised equipment for a radio transmitter and a hospital as a gift. The radio transmitter may have been delivered, and the Russians were certainly involved in the construction of a hospital in 1975, but nothing seems to have come of the hydro-electric station and it has not therefore been included in the totals. Nothing further seems to have been agreed between the two countries on economic co-operation until the 1976 agreement for the cattle-breeding stations and the 1977 credit for projects in the construction industry.

The 1962 agreement was recorded in the official communiqué published in the Soviet foreign trade journal (No. 2, 1963); the details come from Müller. The 1976 agreement has been pieced together from Laotian broadcasts in August; and the 1977 agreement from a Laotian broadcast of 19 July and Vilaggazdasag of 23 July.

Note E: For the reason mentioned above this figure has not been included either in the 'loans outstanding' line or in the totals.

		T	55	56	57	58	59	60	61	62	63	64	65	66	67	68	69	70	71	72	73	74	75	76	77	78	79	80	81	82	83	55-83
Hydroelectric project on the Nam Nien River	*A	34								3.9E																						3.9E
	D																															
	R	12																														
	I	2½																														
	LO																															
Three cattle breeding centres	*A	80																						43								43
	D	50																							1	2	2	3	10	20	5	43
	R	–																													1	1
	I																															
	LO																								43	42	40	38	35	25	5	0
Credit for cement works and brick works	*A	59																							20							20
	D	20																								1	5	10	4	1	1	20
	R	–																													1	2
	I																															
	LO																									20	19	14	4	0		
T O T A L S	A									3.9E														43	20							63
	D																									3	7	13	14	20	5	63
	R																														2	3
	I																															
	LO																								43	62	59	52	39	25	5	0
Soviet Foreign Trade Statistics	D																									0.1	5.7	10.8	16.9	29.7	29.1	92.3

MADAGASCAR

The first Soviet trade agreement with Madagascar was signed in 1964, but diplomatic relations were not opened until 1972. An economic co-operation agreement was signed in 1975, aimed at the field of cement production, and equipment for the university and for a school of navigation. This agreement served as the basis for all subsequent agreements covered in this period; the first protocol in 1977 added mention of a flour mill, a grain silo, and a radio station; the exchange of letters based on it in 1979 expanded the educational theme; and a major credit in 1980 concentrated on road development. Two protocols not shown in the table were for debt rescheduling and for the construction of other projects under unallocated credits from previous protocols. A new credit was agreed in 1982 for the supply of Soviet goods to Madagascar to help defray local expenses.

All agreements were published in the Soviet Treaty series. No account has been taken in the table for debt rescheduling, since the dates, timing, and allocation of the debts into co-operation, trade, and perhaps even military categories would be unreliable. These payments therefore are theoretical.

Item		T	55	56	57	58	59	60	61	62	63	64	65	66	67	68	69	70	71	72	73	74	75	76	77	78	79	80	81	82	83	55-83
Protocol on economic and technical co-operation	A	35																							14							14
	D																															
	R	2 +10																								1	1	1	2	2	2	9
	I	2½																									0.1		0.1	0.1	0.1	0.4
	LO	2½																								14	13	12	11	9	7	5
Exchange of letters on ext'n of co-operation in founding training centres	A	35																									3					3
	D																										2	1				3
	R	2 +10																										0.3	0.3	0.3	0.3	1.2
	I	2½																										0.1		0.1		0.2
	LO	2½																										1	0			
Protocol on continuation of road construction in Madagascar	*A	35																										40				40
	D																												2	10	12	24
	R	2 +10																														
	I	2½																											0.1	0.1	0.3	0.4
	LO	2½																											40	38	28	16
Protocol on economic and technical co-operation	A	32																										40		6	6	6
	D																											2		6		2
	R	2 +10																														2
	I	3																								1						
	LO																								14		3		4		6	4
T O T A L S	A																								14		3	40	4	6	6	63
	D																									1	3	2				38
	R																											0.3	0.3	0.3	0.4	1.2
	I																										0.1	0.1	0.1	0.3	0.4	1.0
	LO																									14	13	13	51	47	41	25

MALI

The first Soviet–Mali economic co-operation agreement was signed in March 1961. It was to encompass geological prospecting for oil, gold, diamonds, and materials for cement production; to improve navigation on the Niger; to provide a stadium at Bamako; to build a railway to Guinea; to construct a cement works; and to provide a teaching centre. A new agreement on the same terms in the following year was to set up a national organization for the management of the Niger river. In 1967 a protocol to the original agreement offered new credits for the projects already under way, providing for local costs for Soviet organizations and for geological prospecting. The same protocol provided credits for covering more local costs in geological prospecting, and for some equipment for the cement works.

All agreements were published in the Soviet Treaty series. The 1967 rescheduling has not been taken into account in the tables since the figures are comparatively small. Repayments and interest payments after 1967 are therefore theoretical.

Agreement / Protocol		T	55	56	57	58	59	60	61	62	63	64	65	66	67	68	69	70	71	72	73	74	75	76	77	78	79	80	81	82	83	55-83
Agreement on economic and technical co-operation	A	34							44																							44
	D									10	12	14	3	2																		44
	R	12													4	4	4	4	4	4	3	3	3	3	3	3						44
	I	2½								0.1	0.2	0.2	0.3	0.4	0.4	0.4	0.4	0.4	0.4	0.4	0.4	0.4	0.4	0.4	0.4	0.4						6.0
	LO									41	31	19	5	2	0																	
Agreement to develop 'Office du Niger'	A	34								11																						11
	D									4	4	3																				11
	R	12												1	1	1	1	1	1	1	1	1	1	1								11
	I	2½									0.1	0.1	0.1	0.2	0.2	0.2	0.2	0.2	0.1	0.1	0.1	0.1	0.1	0.1								2.0
	LO										7	3	0																			
Protocol between Government of USSR and Government of Mali Republic (i)	A	55													6																	6
	D															4	2															6
	R	3 +12																		0.5	0.5	0.5	0.5	0.5	0.5	0.5	0.5	0.5	0.5	0.5	0.5	6.0
	I	–																														
	LO															6	2	0														
Protocol between Government of USSR and Government of Mali Republic (ii)	A	59													7																	7
	D														7																	7
	R	4 +12																		0.5	0.6	0.6	0.6	0.6	0.6	0.6	0.6	0.6	0.6	0.6	0.6	7.0
	I	–																														
	LO																															
Protocol on economic and technical co-operation	A	25																										5				5
	D																											2	2	1		5
	R	10																														0.5
	I	4																											0.1	0.1	0.2	0.4
	LO																												3	1	0	

	T	55	56	57	58	59	60	61	62	63	64	65	66	67	68	69	70	71	72	73	74	75	76	77	78	79	80	81	82	83	55-83
TOTALS A								44	11	16	17	3	2	13	4	2											5	2	1		73
D								3	14			3	2	7	4	2											2	2	1		73
R												1.0	3.0	5.0	5.0	5.0	5.0	5.0	5.0	5.0	5.1	5.1	5.1	4.1	4.1	1.1	1.1	1.1	1.1	1.6	68.5
I									0.1	0.1	0.3	0.4	0.6	0.6	0.6	0.6	0.6	0.5	0.5	0.5	0.5	0.5	0.5	0.5	0.4			0.1	0.1	0.2	8.4
LO									41	38	22	5	2	0	6	2	0											3	1	0	
Soviet Foreign Trade Statistics D									0.6	2.7	3.4	4.1	2.5	3.8	5.2	3.7	2.1	0.9		1.0	0.4	0.6	2.2	2.9	2.0	2.4	1.4				41.9

MONGOLIA

Soviet economic co-operation with Mongolia has been close since well before the Second World War, and it has proved impossible to exclude the latest pre-1954 agreements since they run into the period covered in the tables. The Russians claimed to have provided $225m between 1947 and 1956, and they certainly extended a new credit in 1957 for $61m. In 1961 they offered a massive $500m credit to help finance Mongolia's development in 1961–65, and mentioned the sum of $733m for 1966–70, although in the event this latter was apparently somewhat scaled down. From this period on, all Soviet credits were offered for each successive Mongolian Five Year Plan except the two comparatively small ones offered to celebrate the fiftieth anniversary of the Mongolian Revolution. There is little information on the uses to which the Mongolians have put these very large credits.

The pre-1964 agreements were given in Goldman—the terms are assumed to have been the same as those normally offered later. Although some agreements covered the rescheduling of debts, this has not been taken into account in the tables since it would be difficult to allocate such payments correctly and they do not make much difference to the overall picture; the interest and repayments are therefore theoretical.

It has been noted earlier (p. xvi) that, since one credit—that for 5m roubles in 1969—was stated to be in foreign trade roubles, by implication the other agreements are in domestic Soviet roubles. No differentiation has been made in the table, however.

Note F: Refers to previous years.

Item		T	55	56	57	58	59	60	61	62	63	64	65	66	67	68	69	70	71	72	73	74	75	76	77	78	79	80	81	82	83	55-83
Estimated total credits, drawings etc. until 1956 (F refers to previous years)	*A	41		225F																												225
	D			215F																												225
	R	15		145F	10	10	10	10	10	10	10	10																				225
	I	2		24 F	2	2	2	2	1	1	1	1																				36
	LO	2				55	35	15	5	0																						
Development credit	*A	41			61																												61
	D				6	20	20	10	5																								61
	R	15												4	4	4	5	4	4	4	4	4	4	4	4	4	4	4				61
	I	2			0.1	0.2	0.3	0.4	0.5	0.7	0.7	0.7	0.7	0.7	0.7	0.7	0.7	0.7	0.7	0.6	0.6	0.6	0.6	0.6								11.5
	LO	2																														
1961-65 Development credit	*A	41							500																								500
	D								20	100	110	110	140	20																			500
	R	15												33	33	33	33	33	33	33	33	33	33	34	34	34	34	34				500
	I	2							1.0	1.5	2.0	3.0	4.5	5.4	5.4	5.4	5.4	5.4	5.4	5.4	5.4	5.4	5.4	5.4	5.4	5.4	5.4	5.4				93.0
	LO	2								480	380	270	160	20	0																	
Agreement on ext'n of additional econ'c and tech'l co-operation in 1964/65	*A	33										25																				25
	D											8	10	7																			25
	R	10												2.0	2.0	2.0	2.0	2.0	2.0	2.0	3.0	3.0	3.0	2.0								25
	I	2										0.2	0.3	0.3	0.3	0.3	0.3	0.3	0.2	0.2	0.2	0.2	0.2	0.2								3.2
	LO	2											17	7																		
Agreement on economic and technical co-operation for 1966-70 (i)	*A	41											522																			522
	D												22	100	140	140	100	20														522
	R	15												6	8	9	10	12	48	48	48	48	48	48	48	47	47	47				522
	I	2											2.0	2.4	3.0	4.0	5.0	5.6	5.6	5.6	5.6	5.6	5.6	5.6	5.6	5.6	5.6	5.6				78
	LO	2												500	400	260	120	20	0													
Agreement on economic and technical co-operation for 1966-70 (ii)	*A	100											28																			28
	D													8	10	10																28
	R	-																														-
	I	-																														-
	LO													20	10	0																

Description		T	55	56	57	58	59	60	61	62	63	64	65	66	67	68	69	70	71	72	73	74	75	76	77	78	79	80	81	82	83	55-83
Agr't on projects & supplies of consumer goods for Mongolia's 50th anniversary (i)	A	100															6															6
	D																	3	3													6
	R	-																														
	I	-																														
	LO																															
Agr't on projects & supplies of consumer goods for Mongolia's 50th anniversary (ii)	A	38															11															11
	D																	5	3													11
	R	13																	0.2	0.3	0.5	1.0	1.0	1.0	1.0	1.0	1.0	1.0	1.0	1.0		11
	I	2																	0.1	0.1	0.1	0.1	0.1	0.1	0.1	0.1	0.1	0.1	0.1	0.1	0.1	1.4
	LO																			0												
Agreement on extension of econ'c and tech'l co-operation for 1971-75	A	41																633														633
	D																		33	130	150	160	140	20								633
	R	15																						42	42	42	42	42	42	42	42	336
	I	2																	0.6	1.0	3.0	5.0	6.0	6.8	6.8	6.8	6.8	6.8	6.8	6.8	6.8	70.0
	LO																		633	600	470	320	160	20	0							
Protocol to Agreement of 28th Dec 1970 on economic co-operation	A	41																			19											19
	D																				10	9										19
	R	15																							1.3	1.3	1.3	1.3	1.3	1.3	1.2	9.0
	I	2																			0.2	0.2	0.2	0.2	0.2	0.2	0.2	0.2	0.2	0.2	0.2	2.0
	LO																				9											
Agreement on econ'c and tech'l co-operation for FYP 1976-80 (i)	A	41																					1363									1363
	D																						63	250	300	320	350	80				1363
	R	15																										90	90	91	271
	I	2																					1	3	5	8	12	15	15	15	74
	LO																							1300	1050	750	430	80	0			
Agreement on econ'c and tech'l co-operation for FYP 1976-80 (ii)	A	69																					205									205
	D																						25	40	40	50	50					205
	R	30																													-
	I	-																													-
	LO																							180	140	100	50	0				

		T	55	56	57	58	59	60	61	62	63	64	65	66	67	68	69	70	71	72	73	74	75	76	77	78	79	80	81	82	83	55-83
Agreement on econ'c and tech'l co-operation for FYP 1976-80 (iii)	A	100																														59
	D																							11	12	12	12	12				59
	R	-																														
	I	-																														
	LO																								48	36	24	12	0			
Agreement on econ'c and tech'l co-operation for FYP 1981-85 (i)	A	51																										553	553			553
	D																												53	100	100	253
	R	15																														◆
	I	-																														
	LO																												553	500	400	300
Agreement on econ'c and tech'l co-operation for FYP 1981-85 (ii)	A	36																										2766				2766
	D																												366	600	600	1566
	R	12																											3	8	15	26
	I	2																											2766	2400	1800	1200
	LO																															
Agreement on econ'c and tech'l co-operation for FYP 1981-85 (iii)	A	100																										553				
	D																												15	15	16	46
	R	-																										77				
	I	-																														
	LO																												77	62	47	31
TOTALS	A			225F	61				500			25	550	137	150	140	17	633	36	130	150	170	149	1627	302	352	382	412	3396	514	715	716	7053
	D			215F	9	23	23	11	25	100	110	118	180	137	150	140	106	28	36	130	150	170	149	119	302	352	382	412	514	715	716	5522
	R			145F	10	10	10	10	10	14	14	14	4	45	47	48	50	51	87	88	89	89	89	131	126	125	125	125	134	134	134	1960
	I			24 F	2.1	2.2	2.3	2.4	2.5	3.2	3.7	4.9	7.5	8.8	9.4	10.4	11.5	12.1	12.6	12.9	14.9	17.1	18.1	19.9	21.1	23.1	26.1	30.1	25.1	30.1	37.0	395.1
	LO			10	10	62	39	16	5	480	380	270	177	547	410	260	120	31	636	600	470	320	169	20	1528	1226	874	492	3476	2962	2247	1531
Soviet Foreign Trade Statistics	D			2.7	5.3	6.7	5.8	10.6	13.1	11.8	28.4	29.9	33.8	36.3	57.2	72.1	81.4	86.3	80.0	104	129	165	226	337	409	498	465	557	502	593	625	5170

MOROCCO

The first Soviet–Moroccan trade agreement was signed in 1958, and, according to Goldman, Morocco received some military aid from the Soviet Union in 1962. The first economic co-operation agreement was signed in 1966. It was in two parts: the first, for 17m roubles, was for the construction of a metal-working complex in Casablanca and the construction of the Nur Baz dam and hydro-electric power station; the second, with a slightly shorter life, was for 15m roubles for the construction of a lead–zinc plant at Bu-Madina.

1974 saw the start of a series of discussions and agreements on the development of the massive Meskala phosphate deposit, involving the sum of $2,000m. It was generally agreed that the Soviet Union would finance all the overseas costs, which would be repaid in phosphate deliveries to the USSR and East Europe, while the Moroccans would meet the local costs. Two agreements appear to have been signed under this heading: the first was the allocation of a $250 credit in 1977 to the 'Office Cherifien des Phosphates' for the development of a new Atlantic port for phosphate exports; the second was for $20m in 1978 for geological prospecting and feasibility studies as part of a long-term agreement on phosphate exploitation. Little work appears to have been started under either of these agreements by the end of 1983.

All agreements were published in the Soviet Treaty series except the 1977 agreement, which was reported in *Vilaggazdasag* of 4 June 1977 and *Industrie- und Handelsblatt* of 4 July 1977.

	T	55	56	57	58	59	60	61	62	63	64	65	66	67	68	69	70	71	72	73	74	75	76	77	78	79	80	81	82	83	55–83
Agreement on economic and technical co-operation (i)																															
A	34												19																		19
D																															19
R	12													1	1	3	3	5	4	1	1	2	2	2	2	2	1	1	1	1	19
I	24															0.1	0.1	0.2	0.3	0.3	0.3	0.3	0.3	0.3	0.2	0.2	0.2	0.2	0.2	0.2	3.4
LO														19	18	17	14	11	6	2	1	0									
Agreement on economic and technical co-operation (cont'd) (ii)																															
A	27												17																		17
D																															17
R	8													1	1	2	2	3	5	1	1	1	2	2	2	2	2				17
I	24																0.1		0.2	0.3	0.3	0.2	0.2	0.2	0.2	0.2	0.2				2.2
LO	24													17	16	15	13	11	8	3	2	1	0								
Long term agreement on development of 1st stage of Meskala phosphate deposit																															
+A	43																							250							250
D	20																								20						6
R	20																								1	1	1	1	1	1	5
I	24																								250	249	248	247	246	245	244
LO	24																								250	249	248	247	246	245	244
Long term agreement on economic and tech'l co-op'n in sphere of phosphates																															
A	36																								20						20
D																															5
R	3 +12																									1	1	1	1	1	5
I	24																									20	19	18	17	16	15
LO	34																									20	19	18	17	16	15
TOTALS																															
A													36											250	20						306
D															2	1	1	1	1	4	5	4	4	4	4	4	3	1	1	1	47
R														2	2	5	5	8	9	2	2	1	4	4	4	4	3	1	1	1	36
I															0.1	0.1	0.1	0.3	0.5	0.6	0.6	0.5	0.5	0.5	0.4	0.4	0.4	0.2	0.2	0.2	5.6
LO														36	34	32	27	22	14	5	3	1	0	0	250	269	267	265	263	261	259
Soviet Foreign Trade Statistics																															
D																5.3	4.7		8.6	2.3	1.0	0.1	0.1	0.1	…	…					22.2

MOZAMBIQUE

The first mention of Soviet economic co-operation with Mozambique was made by a visiting Soviet delegation from Dar-es-Salaam in 1975; in the following year the Russians agreed to extend a credit of 10m roubles for feasibility and pre-investment studies, the delivery of equipment for a technical school and a hospital, and geological prospecting. The amount was increased in 1979 for 'agricultural and industrial development' with mention of a particular project—an aluminium works at Sofala. Subsequent agreements in 1980 and 1982 were also for a wide range of projects—a tractor assembly plant, cotton growing, coal prospecting and mining, experimental agricultural stations, rural electrification, drilling for oil and gas and water, and further feasibility studies.

All agreements were in the Soviet Treaty series except the second. This was referred to in the third agreement, which 'raised credits under the 1976 and 1979 (sic) agreements from 31m to 42m roubles'; the 1979 agreement must therefore have been of a value of 21m roubles to make the 1976 agreement up to 31m roubles.

Agreement		T	55	56	57	58	59	60	61	62	63	64	65	66	67	68	69	70	71	72	73	74	75	76	77	78	79	80	81	82	83	55-83
Protocol to Agreement on economic and technical co-operation	A	34																							14								14
	D																																
	R	12																							2	7	5	1	1	1	1	1	5
	I	24																								0.1	0.2	0.2	0.3	0.2	0.3	0.2	1.5
	LO																									12	5	0					
Protocol to Agreement on economic and tech'l co-op'n of 12th Feb 1976	*A	34																										32					32
	D																												18	11	3		32
	R	12																													3	3	6
	I	24																											0.2	0.4	0.4	0.4	1.5
	LO																												29	11	0	0	
Protocol to Agreement on economic and tech'l co-op'n of 12th Feb 1976	A	34																											19				19
	D																												3	10	6		19
	R	12																														1.5	1.5
	I	24																											0.1	0.2	0.3	0.3	0.7
	LO																													16	6	0	
Protocol to Agreement on economic and tech'l co-op'n of 12th Feb 1976	A	29																											5				5
	D																												2	2	3		5
	R	10																													0.5	0.5	1.0
	I	3																												0.1	0.1	0.1	0.2
	LO																												5	3	6	0	
Agreement on development of economic and technical co-operation	A	32																											108				108
	D																												2	20	60	20	102
	R	2 +10																												0.5	1.0	1.7	3.2
	I	3																												0.1	0.5	0.1	6
	LO																													106	86	26	

	T	55	56	57	58	59	60	61	62	63	64	65	66	67	68	69	70	71	72	73	74	75	76	77	78	79	80	81	82	83	55-83
Protocol to Agreement of 18th Nov 1980																															
A	32																												96		96
D																													10	30	40
R	2 +10																														
I	3																													1	1
LO																														86	56
TOTALS																															
A																							14			32	132		96		274
D																							2	7	5	3	25	44	76	50	212
R																										1.0	1.0	1.0	4.5	6.0	13.5
I																								0.1	0.2	0.3	0.5	1.3	2.0	3.7	8.1
LO																								12	5	5	29	136	92	112	62

NEPAL

The first Soviet–Nepalese economic agreement was for Soviet 'assistance' (pomoshch') rather than co-operation. Under it Nepal received as a gift from the USSR three projects valued at 30m old roubles: a cigarette factory at Janakpur, completed in 1964; the Birjing sugar factory, completed in January 1965; and the Pananti 1200kW hydro-electric power station, completed in October 1965. There is no information on the value of three other projects undertaken by the Russians at the same time: a pediatric hospital in Kathmandu, completed in 1963; an agricultural implements factory in Birjing, completed in 1968; and the Janakpur–Simla road, completed at the end of 1972.

A 1961 agreement to which Goldman refers—a credit for $2\frac{1}{2}$m new roubles—was repayable in five years at $2\frac{1}{2}$% interest and was not therefore on 'aid' terms.

A general new co-operation agreement was announced in 1976; it gave rise to the 1978 agreement on the construction of a resin and turpentine factory roughly on the standard Soviet economic co-operation terms. It was completed in 1981, and there has been no active Soviet economic co-operation activity since.

Both the agreements in the table were published in the Soviet Treaty series.

		T	55	56	57	58	59	60	61	62	63	64	65	66	67	68	69	70	71	72	73	74	75	76	77	78	79	80	81	82	83	55-83
Agreement on extension of economic and technical assistance	A	100					8																									8
	D						8																									8
	R	-																														
	I	-																														
	LO							8	8	7	6	5	4	3	2	0																
Agreement on economic and technical co-operation	A	41																								4.4						4.4
	D																										1.4	2.0	1.0			4.4
	R	3+12																												...	0.3	0.3
	I	24																											0.1	0.0	0.1	0.2
	LO																										4.4	3.0	1.0	0.0		
T O T A L S	A						8																			4.4						12.4
	D								1.0	1.0	1.0	1.0	1.0	1.0	2.0												1.4	2.0	1.0			12.4
	R																														0.3	0.3
	I																												0.1	0.1		0.2
	LO							8	8	7	6	5	4	3	2	0											4.4	3.0	1.0	0.0		
Soviet Foreign Trade Statistics	D																	0.8														0.8

NICARAGUA

The first Soviet economic assistance to Nicaragua came in 1981 in the form of a grant for the emergency purchase of commodities after the disastrous floods of 1981. It was reported by Managua radio in 1982 that the credit was mainly used for the purchase of materials and equipment for the chemical industry—iron, urea, and ammonia. Later in the same year the Russians offered a development loan for agriculture; the terms were not given, but are assumed to be of the same order as later credits. In 1982 a trade credit was offered for the purchase of heavy equipment, and soon after another credit was destined for, among other things, feasibility studies for a dam and hydro-electric power station at Capala, equipment for a hospital, and geological prospecting for gold and other minerals. A protocol signed two weeks later referred specifically to the development of the hydro-electric power station. The 1983 agreement was to increase cotton yarn production and to establish a bread factory.

The first agreement was widely reported later in the media—for example, Managua Radio on 22 July 1982, *Barricada* (Managua) on 2 September 1982. The second agreement was also widely reported, with full details given by the Nicaraguan leader Ortega to Managua Radio, which broadcast them on 10 May 1982. The $100m trade credit was reported in *La Prensa* of 23 August 1982 and Managua Radio on 14 November and 17 December 1982, and confirmed indirectly by the Soviet ambassador's statement over Managua Radio that total Soviet credits up to then (1 November 1982) amounted to $180m. The other three were published in the Soviet Treaty series.

		T	55	56	57	58	59	60	61	62	63	64	65	66	67	68	69	70	71	72	73	74	75	76	77	78	79	80	81	82	83	55-83
Emergency commodity grant	*A	100																											31			31
	D																															
	R	-																														
	I	-																											16	15		31
	LO																															
Development loan for agriculture	*A	35																											50			50
	D																													25	25	50
	R	2 +12																														
	I	3																												0.4	0.8	1.2
	LO	3																												50	25	0
Trade credit	*A	31																												100		100
	D																													10	40	50
	R	3 +10																														
	I	4																												0.2	0.8	1.0
	LO	4																													90	50
Agreement on economic and technical co-operation	A	36																												48		48
	D																													5	30	35
	R	2 +10																														
	I	3																												0.1	0.5	0.6
	LO	3																													43	13
Protocol to Agreement on econ'c and tech'l co-operation of 5th Oct 1976	A	31																												4		4
	D																														2	2
	R	3 +10																														
	I	4																														
	LO	4																													4	2

		T	55	56	57	58	59	60	61	62	63	64	65	66	67	68	69	70	71	72	73	74	75	76	77	78	79	80	81	82	83	55-83
Agreement on economic and technical co-operation	A	32																													20	20
	D																															
	R	2 +10																														
	I	3																														
	LO																															20
T O T A L S	A																												81	152	20	253
	D																												16	55	97	168
	R																															
	I																													0.7	2.1	2.8
	LO																													65	162	85

NIGERIA

The first Soviet economic co-operation agreement was signed in 1961; it was a credit of 40m new roubles to provide assistance in agriculture, manufacturing plant, and an educational centre, though there is little evidence of this credit having been taken up. A 1968 agreement acted as the framework for future agreements, and the 1970 credit for a 6m rouble credit was based on it: it was for geological prospecting and equipment for laboratories, and the terms of 3% interest with repayment in eight years just bring it into the 'aid' category. The massive support being given to the development of Nigeria's iron and steel plant is not on 'aid' terms.

The original credit was recorded in Müller; the second was published in the Soviet Treaty series.

	T	55	56	57	58	59	60	61	62	63	64	65	66	67	68	69	70	71	72	73	74	75	76	77	78	79	80	81	82	83	55-83
Credit for various projects																															
+A	34							45																							45
D									1	1	1	1	1																		5
R	12													0.3	0.3	0.3	0.4	0.4	0.4	0.4	0.4	0.4	0.4	0.4	0.4	0.5					5.0
I	2½												0.1		0.1					0.1											0.3
LO									45	44	43	42	41	40	40	40	40	40	40	40	40	40	40	40	40	40	40	40	40	40	40
Protocol to Agreement on econ'c and tech'l co-operation of 21st Dec 1968																															
A	25																7														7
D																		1	2	2	1	1									7
R	8																					0.5	0.5	1.0	1.0	1.0	1.0	1.0	1.0		7.0
I	3																			0.1	0.1	0.2	0.1	0.1	0.1	0.1	0.1	0.1	0.1		1.1
LO																		1	3	5	6	6	6	5	4	3	2	1	0		
TOTALS																															
A								45									7														52
D									1	1	1	1	1					1	2	2	1	1									12
R														0.3	0.3	0.3	0.4	0.4	0.4	0.4	0.4	0.9	0.9	1.4	1.4	1.5	1.0	1.0	1.0		12.0
I													0.1		0.1					0.2	0.1	0.2	0.1	0.1	0.1	0.1	0.1	0.1	0.1		1.4
LO									45	44	43	42	41	40	40	40	40	41	43	45	46	46	46	45	44	43	42	41	40	40	40
Soviet Foreign Trade Statistics																															
D																	1.8		0	1	1	1	0	8	68	31	99	188	354	379	1133

PAKISTAN

Diplomatic relations between Karachi and Moscow were opened in July 1954. In 1958 discussions were held between the two countries on the possibility of Soviet economic assistance in agriculture and in the construction of a steel mill, but the 1961 agreement on co-operation in oil and gas prospecting was apparently the first to be signed. In 1965 the Russians offered a general credit for Pakistani purchases of Soviet goods at world prices; the terms given in the tables are the best offered, with the interest ranging between $2\frac{1}{2}$ and $3\frac{1}{2}$%. An \$11m credit in the same year for assistance in agriculture was not on 'aid' terms. The first credit in 1966 was for the purchase of equipment and materials for an electrical equipment factory, a thermal power station, fifteen radio transmitters, a 1200km high tension line, a road and rail bridge, and geological prospecting, and for Soviet technical assistance. The second credit in the same year was for the construction of an airport. In 1968 a new agreement increased the first 1966 credit by 100m Pakistani rupees in 1969 and 220m in 1970.

In 1970 the first agreement was signed for the development of the Pipri iron and steel works near Karachi; a total of over \$500m in credits represented the Soviet contribution to this plant by the end of 1980, and it went into production in March 1983. Another major plant with which the Soviet Union was connected was the Guddu thermal electric power station in Baluchistan; the first two 110MW sets had been installed by the Czechs, but the Soviet Union agreed in 1973 to provide the credits and equipment for a single 220MW set on this site. It started producing electricity in 1980.

Information on the first credit came from Goldman, and on the airport from the FES series. The rest were published in the Soviet Treaty series.

A 1973 agreement rescheduled part of Pakistan's debts, and discussed the exchange rate on which repayments and interest were based, but this could not be represented in the tables and these payments are therefore theoretical.

Pakistan government statistics on economic aid are, like India's, more complete than most, and their own figures for Soviet credits are shown in the last section of the tables; the A line shows annual credits, the A(i) line the five-year credits (all years are financial—July to June). For the purpose of consistency the official Soviet Treaty series is taken as priority; but an example of the complication of compiling these

Description		T	55	56	57	58	59	60	61	62	63	64	65	66	67	68	69	70	71	72	73	74	75	76	77	78	79	80	81	82	83	55‑83
Oil and gas prospecting	*A	34							30																							30
	D									30																						30
	R	12												2.5	2.5	2.5	2.5	2.5	2.5	2.5	2.5	2.5	2.5	2.5	2.5							30
	I	2½												0.4	0.4	0.4	0.4	0.4	0.4	0.4	0.4	0.4	0.4	0.4	0.4							4.8
	LO									30	30	18	16	14	12	10	8	6	4	2	0											
Protocol on deliveries of machinery and equipment	*A	31											32																			32
	D													2	10	17	3															32
	R	10														3	3	3	3	3	3	3	3	4	4							32
	I	2½												0.4	0.4	0.4	0.4	0.4	0.4	0.4	0.4	0.4	0.5	0.5	0.5							4.3
	LO													30	20	3	0															
Agreement on economic and technical co‑operation	*A	34												22																		22
	D														10	10	2															22
	R	12																1.9	1.9	1.9	1.8	1.8	1.8	1.8	1.8	1.8	1.8	1.8	1.8			22
	I	2½													0.1	0.3	0.3	0.3	0.3	0.3	0.3	0.3	0.3	0.3	0.3	0.3	0.3	0.3				4.0
	LO														22	12	2	0														
Airport	*A	30															21	3														3
	D																															
	R	6																6	6	6												3
	I	–																														–
	LO														3	3	3	3														
Agreement on co‑operation in searching and prospecting for oil and gas	*A	34																											21			21
	D																					215										21
	R	12																	6		1.8	1.8	1.8	1.8	1.8	1.8	1.8	1.8	1.7	1.7	1.7	19.5
	I	2½																0.1	0.2	0.3	0.3	0.3	0.3	0.3	0.3	0.3	0.3	0.3	0.3	0.3	0.2	3.8
	LO																	18	12	6	0											
Agree't on ext'n of economic and tech'l co‑op'n in constr'n of State iron and steel wks	*A	34																	247	32		215										515
	D																				2	8	10	15	30	60	125	110	55	50	50	515
	R	12																										10	20	30	35	35	140
	I	2½																										2	2	4	6	7	28
	LO																		247	247	279	277	484	474	459	429	369	244	134	100	50	0

statistics is that the Pakistan statistics omit the 1973 credit mainly for Guddu, and include the 1983 credit which was repayable in twelve years at $5\frac{1}{2}\%$ interest, a grant element well below the 'aid' level.

	T	55	56	57	58	59	60	61	62	63	64	65	66	67	68	69	70	71	72	73	74	75	76	77	78	79	80	81	82	83	55-83
Protocol to Agreement on econ'c and tech'l co-operation of 9th Sept 1966 — A	34																														71
Protocol — D																															
Protocol — R	12																					6	20	40	5						71
Protocol — I	24																							6	6	6	6	6	6	6	42
Protocol — LO																								1	1	1	1	1	1	1	7
TOTALS — A								30				32	25			21		247	32	71	215							21			694
TOTALS — D										12	2	4	12	29	15	7	11	8	8	2	8	16	35	70	65	125	110	55	50	50	694
TOTALS — R													2.5	2.5	5.5	7.4	7.4	7.4	7.9	9.6	9.6	9.6	10.6	16.6	19.6	19.6	29.6	37.7	42.7	42.7	288.5
TOTALS — I													0.4	0.5	1.1	1.1	1.2	1.3	1.4	1.4	1.4	1.5	1.5	2.5	3.6	3.6	5.6	7.3	8.3	8.2	51.9
TOTALS — LO									30	30	18	16	44	57	28	13	27	16	255	279	348	555	539	504	434	369	244	134	100	50	0
Pakistan Gov't Statistics — A																		247			215		0.1		106		14.5	21.4		284	923.5
Pakistan Gov't Statistics — A (i)							I<—		35.9			—>I<—			78.4		—>I		32			3.5									
Soviet Foreign Trade Statistics — D													0.3	0.6	4.2	8.6	7.9	11.1	2.4	3.4	8.5	24.7	38.3	68.9	67.8	158	141	59.0	58.8	63.2	726.1
Soviet Foreign Trade Statistics — A																															

PERU

The Soviet Union and Peru reopened diplomatic relations in May 1969 after an interval. The new Peruvian ambassador to Moscow, Javier Perez de Cuellar, started discussions at an early stage on the possibility of Soviet co-operation in the construction of an irrigation network at Olmos in the Andes, 900km north of Lima, and already in January there had been talk of a long-term low-interest credit. The agreement signed in August 1970, however, made no mention of Olmos, the credit being offered for 'machinery and equipment' in general; and the next credit, in 1971, was for a fish processing factory (fishmeal being a major Peruvian export to the USSR and East Europe) and for assistance in mining.

In 1977 the first credit for Olmos was advanced—a feasibility study for the dam, the irrigation scheme, and the hydro-electric power station—and in April 1980 the Russians extended a credit of $300m out of a total estimated cost of $700m with the suggestion that other East European countries might offer credits. The new Peruvian government, however, asked for a revision of the terms, and in 1981 a consortium of companies from Brazil, Italy, Sweden, and the USA also became involved. Early in 1983 the Soviet ambassador in Lima said that the Soviet Union would abide by its undertaking, but by the end of the year no further progress appears to have been made.

Only the first agreement appeared in the Soviet Treaty series; the second came from *Marktinformationen* of 20 September 1971 and *BfA/NfA* (J) of 18 October 1971; the third was mentioned in *Latin American Round-up* of 28 June 1977; and the major agreement on Olmos appeared in the press passim—for example, *La Prensa* on 25 May 1980 and Paris Radio in Spanish in 12 July 1980.

Project	Item	T	55	56	57	58	59	60	61	62	63	64	65	66	67	68	69	70	71	72	73	74	75	76	77	78	79	80	81	82	83	55-83
Agreement on deliveries of machinery and equipment	A	29																30														30
	D																				5	10	15									30
	R	10																						3	3	3	3	3	3	3	3	24
	I	3																			0.1	0.2	0.4	0.5	0.5	0.5	0.5	0.5	0.5	0.5	0.5	4.7
	LO																			30	30	25	15	0								
Fish processing factory	+A	29																	30													30
	D																					2	18	8								30
	R	10																							3	3	3	3	3	3	3	21
	I	3																					0.2	0.3	0.5	0.5	0.5	0.5	0.5	0.5	0.5	4.0
	LO	3																		30	30	30	28	10	2	0						
Feasibility studies for Olmos HEP	+A	29																								1						1
	D																								1							1
	R	10																									0.1	0.1	0.1	0.1	0.1	0.5
	I	3																										0.1				0.1
	LO																									1	0					
Olmos hydroelectric project	+A	30																										300	300	300	300	300
	D																															
	R	7+18																														
	I	6½																														
	LO																															
T O T A L S	A																	30	30							1		300	300	300	300	361
	D																				5	12	33	8	1							61
	R																							3.0	6.0	6.0	6.1	6.1	6.1	6.1	6.1	45.5
	I																				0.1	0.2	0.6	0.8	1.0	1.0	1.0	1.1	1.0	1.0	1.0	8.8
	LO																			60	60	55	43	10	2	1						300

SAO TOMÉ E PRINCIPÉ

The Soviet Union signed a fisheries agreement with Sao Tomé e Principé in December 1981, and in May 1982 agreed to a 3m rouble loan towards feasibility studies and tests for the construction of a 6MW hydro-electric power station. The agreement was published in the Soviet Treaty series.

Feasibility study for a hydroelectric power station		T	55	56	57	58	59	60	61	62	63	64	65	66	67	68	69	70	71	72	73	74	75	76	77	78	79	80	81	82	83	55-83
	A	31																												4		4
	D																														1	1
	R	3 +10																															
	I	4																															
	LO																															4	3

SENEGAL

The first Soviet–Senegalese economic co-operation agreement was signed in 1962, proposing the fields of future Soviet assistance. It was followed in March 1965 by a protocol which specified a credit for the construction of a fish cannery and the delivery of fishing boats. Another protocol in December 1969 diverted some of the same credit towards geological prospecting. These agreements were published in the Soviet Treaty series.

		T	55	56	57	58	59	60	61	62	63	64	65	66	67	68	69	70	71	72	73	74	75	76	77	78	79	80	81	82	83	55-83
Protocol to Agreement on econ'c and tech'l co-operation of 14th June 1962	A	34											6.7																			6.7
	D													0.2	1.0	1.0	1.5	2.0	0.5	0.5												6.7
	R	12																		0.5	0.5	0.5	0.5	0.5	0.6	0.6	0.6	0.6	0.6	0.7		6.7
	I	24														0.1			0.1	0.1	0.1	0.1	0.1	0.1	0.1	0.1	0.1	0.1	0.1			1.2
	LO													6.7	6.5	5.5	4.5	3.0	1.0	0.5	0.0												
Soviet Foreign Trade Statistics	D																	1														1

SIERRA LEONE

In the mid-1960s the Soviet Union offered credits on very favourable terms to many sub-Saharan countries, and Sierra Leone was no exception. The 1967 agreement was for the purchase of Soviet-manufactured agricultural machinery, but there is little evidence of any drawings on this credit. The 1973 credit for hospital equipment was, however, soon taken up.

The first agreement was recorded in the BBC *SWB* No. 439, recording a credit of £20m. The ·second agreement came from several sources—the details in particular were recorded in *Marchés Tropicaux* of 2 March 1973.

		T	55	56	57	58	59	60	61	62	63	64	65	66	67	68	69	70	71	72	73	74	75	76	77	78	79	80	81	82	83	55-83
Credit for the purchase of agricultural machinery	+A	34													48																	48
	D														0.3																	0.3
	R	12																0.1			0.1			0.1								0.3
	I	24																														
	LO															47.7	47.7	47.7	47.7	47.7	47.7	47.7	47.7	47.7	47.7	47.7	47.7	47.7	47.7	47.7	47.7	47.7
Equipment for four hospitals	+A	29																			3											3
	D																				3	3	1	2								3
	R	12																							0.2	0.2	0.2	0.2	0.2	0.2	0.3	1.5
	I	34																							0.1	0.1	0.1	0.1	0.1		0.1	0.4
	LO																					3	3	2	0							
T O T A L S	A														48						3	3	1	2								51
	D														0.3						3											3.3
	R																	0.1			0.1			0.1	0.2	0.2	0.2	0.2	0.2	0.2	0.3	1.8
	I																								0.1	0.1	0.1	0.1	0.1	0.1	0.1	0.4
	LO														47.7	47.7	47.7	47.7	47.7	47.7	50.7	50.7	50.7	49.7	47.7	47.7	47.7	47.7	47.7	47.7	47.7	47.7

SOMALIA

In May 1961 Soviet–Somali talks were held in Moscow on the future of the economic, technical, and cultural relations between the two countries, and in June the first economic co-operation agreement was signed. It was designed to channel Soviet assistance into a wide range of projects such as livestock and cotton state farms, a 2.5MW hydro-electric power station, seaport development, three undertakings in the food industry, geological prospecting for tin and lead, and boring for water. The Soviet Union made a grant (value not specified) in 1962 for equipment for hospitals and schools, and in 1966 a protocol to the 1961 agreement hived off part of the credit for the import of Soviet goods to be sold in Somalia towards defraying some of the local Soviet costs. The next addition to the 1961 credit, in 1971, also included an element for local costs. Two protocols were signed in 1972: the first for the development of the Fanole dam, irrigation scheme, and hydro-electric power station; the second for Somali purchases of agricultural machinery and equipment. In 1975 a protocol mentioning all the previous agreements increased the credits by 7m roubles, of which 3m were to be used to cover local costs.

Apart from the Fanole dam and hydro-electric power station, the main Soviet projects in Somalia were the meat canning factory in Kismayu, on the Juba, a fish cannery at Las Khoreh, the equipment of the Shaykh hospital, and several state farms.

The first four agreements were published in the Soviet Treaty series. The fifth, signed on 16 May 1975, appeared after ratification in *Vedomosti Verkhnogo Soveta* (Moscow) of 28 July 1976, and the last on Radio Mogadishu of 19 June 1975 and *Aussenhandel der UdSSR* of November 1975. Some agreements included rescheduling, and it is likely that there was some disruption in payments after the expulsion of the Soviet experts in 1977; repayments and interest are therefore theoretical.

		T	55	56	57	58	59	60	61	62	63	64	65	66	67	68	69	70	71	72	73	74	75	76	77	78	79	80	81	82	83	55-83
Agreement on economic and technical co-operation	A	38							52																							52
	D																															52
	R	2 +12								2	5	10	15	10	5	3	2	5	5	4	4	4	4	3	3	1						52
	I	2½								0.1	0.2	0.3	0.4	0.7	0.7	0.7	0.7	0.7	0.7	0.7	0.7	0.7	0.7	0.7	0.3							9.0
	LO									52	50	45	35	20	10	5	2	0														
Protocol to Agreement on econ'c and tech'l co-operation of 2nd June 1961	A	38																	6													6
	D																		2	2	2											6
	R	2 +12																		2	2	0.5	0.5	0.5	0.5	0.5	0.5	0.5	0.5	0.5	0.5	5.0
	I	2½																			0.1				0.1	0.1	0.1	0.1	0.1	0.1	0.1	1.0
	LO																	0			2	0										
Protocol to Agreement on econ'c and tech'l co-operation of 2nd June 1961	A	38																		12													12
	D																				2												12
	R	2 +12																				2	4	4	1	1	1	1	1	1	8
	I	2½																				0.1	0.2	0.2	0.2	0.2	0.2	0.2	0.2	0.2	1.9
	LO																				12	12	10	6	2	0						
Agricultural equipment	*A	27																		7												7
	D																															7
	R	8																			1	2	2	2	2	2	0.5	0.6	0.6	0.6	0.6	4.9
	I	2½																				0.1	0.1	0.1	0.1	0.1	0.1	0.1	0.1	0.1	1.0
	LO																				7	6	4	2	0						
Protocol to Agreement on econ'c and tech'l co-operation of 2nd June 1961	*A	38																						9								9
	D																															9
	R	2 +12																						3	4	2		0.8	0.8	0.8	0.8	3.2
	I	2½																							0.1	2	0	0.1	0.1	0.1	0.1	0.6
	LO																						9	6	2	0					
Equipment for the fishing industry and trade credits	*A	38																						64								64
	D																								2	5						7
	R	2 +12																								1	1	1	1	1	1	6
	I	2½																														...
	LO																								64	62	57	57	57	57	57	57

	T	55	56	57	58	59	60	61	62	63	64	65	66	67	68	69	70	71	72	73	74	75	76	77	78	79	80	81	82	83	55–83
T O T A L S	A							52										6	19			9	64								150
	D								2	5	10	15	10	5	3	2	5	2	2	3	4	6	9	8	7						93
	R										1	2	4	4	4	4	4	5	4	4	4.5	5	5	5	4	3	3	3.9	3.9	3.9	79.1
	I								0.1	0.2	0.3	0.4	0.7	0.7	0.7	0.7	0.7	0.7	0.7	0.8	0.9	1.1	1.1	0.7	0.5	0.5	0.5	0.5	0.5	0.5	13.5
	LO								52	50	45	35	20	10	5	2	0		4	21	18	14	17	72	64	57	57	57	57	57	57
Somalia Official Reports on Agreements	A																	3.4					83.4	24.4							111.2
Soviet Foreign Trade Statistics	D																		1.5	3.8	4.2	9.4	10.0	7.9							36.8

SRI LANKA

The first exchange of ambassadors between the USSR and Sri Lanka was agreed in September 1956, and at the same time trade development and economic co-operation were adumbrated. In 1957 the Sri Lankans accepted the offer of Soviet experts to prospect for oil. The first econmic co-operation agreement, signed in February 1958, was offered for irrigation and hydro-technology, and for increasing agricultural and fisheries production; in practice it may also have been used for the first stage of the Oruvela steel works. In 1971 a further credit was extended for the purchase of machinery and equipment, and in 1972 Soviet oil prospecting apparently received its first credit. In 1974 two new credits, on differing terms, were extended for the second and third stages of Oruvela. A major new credit in 1975 was for the construction of the Samanala-Veva dam and hydro-electric power station.

The first and last agreements were published in the Soviet Treaty series. The second was mentioned in *Marktinformationen* No. 16, 1971; the third was in *Vilaggazdasag* of 4 October 1972 and *Blick durch die Wirtschaft* of 11 October 1972; and the two Oruvela credits were pieced together from various press and radio sources—for example, Colombo radio on 29 June 1974 and *Aussenhandel der UdSSR* No. 12, 1974.

Item		T	55	56	57	58	59	60	61	62	63	64	65	66	67	68	69	70	71	72	73	74	75	76	77	78	79	80	81	82	83	55-83
Agreement on economic and technical co-operation	A	34				30																										30
	D									2	3	3	6	6	5	3	2															30
	R	12														2.5	2.5	2.5	2.5	2.5	2.5	2.5	2.5	2.5	2.5	2.5	2.5					30
	I	24												0.5	0.5	0.5	0.5	0.4	0.4	0.4	0.4	0.4	0.4	0.4	0.4	0.4	0.4					6.0
	LO						30	30	30	30	28	25	22	16	10	5	2	0														
Machinery and equipment credit	*A	29																	5													5
	D																			1	1	1	1	1								5
	R	10																						0.5	0.5	0.5	0.5	0.5	0.5	0.5	0.5	4.0
	I	3																			0.1	0.1	0.1	0.1	0.1	0.1	0.1	0.1	0.1	0.1	0.1	1.0
	LO																			5	4	3	2	1	0							
Oil prospecting	*A	29																		5												5
	D																			5	2	2	1									5
	R	10																			0.5	0.5	0.5	0.5	0.5	0.5	0.5	0.5				4.0
	I	3																			0.1	0.1	0.1	0.1	0.1	0.1	0.1	0.1	0.1	0.1	0.1	1.0
	LO																			5	5	3	1	0								
Oruvela Steel stages II and III (i)	*A	29																				2.5										2.5
	D																						0.5	2.0								2.5
	R	10																							0.2	0.2	0.2	0.2	0.2	0.3	0.3	1.6
	I	3																							0.1	0.1	0.1					0.3
	LO																					2.5		0.0								
Oruvela Steel stages II and III (ii)	*A	45																				2.5										2.5
	D																						0.5	2.0								2.5
	R	12																								0.2	0.2	0.2	0.2	0.2	0.2	1.4
	I	-																											0.1			-
	LO																					2.5		2.0	0.0							
Agreement on economic and technical co-operation	A	38																					55									55
	D																															
	R	15																														
	I	24																														
	LO																								55	55	55	55	55	55	55	55	55

	T	55	56	57	58	59	60	61	62	63	64	65	66	67	68	69	70	71	72	73	74	75	76	77	78	79	80	81	82	83	55-83
TOTALS A					30																	55									100
D									2	3	3	6	6	5	3	2			1	3	3	3	5								45
R															2.5	2.5	2.5	2.5	2.5	2.5	2.5	2.5	3.5	3.9	3.9	3.9	1.4	1.4	1.5	1.5	41.0
I													0.5	0.5	0.5	0.5	0.4	0.4	0.4	0.6	0.6	0.6	0.6	0.7	0.6	0.7	0.2	0.3	0.2		8.3
LO						30	30	30	30	28	25	22	16	10	5	2	0		5	9	6	8	60	55	55	55	55	55	55	55	55
Soviet Foreign Trade Statistics D			0.5	…					0.9	2.9	6.8	4.3	0.1	1.1	0.4	0.8	0.3		0.3	3.0	1.1	1.8	3.7	3.1	2.2	1.1		0.9	0.5	0.2	36.0

SUDAN

The first Soviet economic co-operation agreement with the Sudan in 1961 took the form of an open credit, on the standard Soviet terms of $2\frac{1}{2}$% interest repayable in twelve years. The projects considered under this credit were two granaries, four food processing plants, an agricultural research centre, and feasibility studies and pilot schemes. A protocol to this agreement in 1968 reduced the interest on a new credit to 2%, but also reduced the repayment period to eight years; it was for the purchase of machinery and equipment. In the following year a new agreement offered a credit for geological and geophysical prospecting for minerals in the Red Sea mountain range: the terms were $2\frac{1}{2}$% repayable in ten years, and the contract was signed in May 1970.

All the agreements were published in the Soviet Treaty series. The contract for the last agreement was announced on Omdurman radio on 31 May 1970.

	T	55	56	57	58	59	60	61	62	63	64	65	66	67	68	69	70	71	72	73	74	75	76	77	78	79	80	81	82	83	55-83
Agreement on economic and technical co-operation — A	34							22																							22
D																															20
R	12												1.0	1.0	1.0	1.0	1.0	1.2	1.2	1.2	1.2	1.2	1.2	1.6	1.3	1.0	0.7	0.4	0.4	0.4	18.0
I	24												0.1	0.1	0.1	0.2	0.2	0.2	0.2	0.2	0.2	0.2	0.2	0.2	0.2	0.2	0.2	0.2	0.2	0.1	3.4
LO	24								22	21	18	13	11	10	9	8	8	6	6	6	6	6	6	4	3	2	2	2	2	2	2
Protocol on deliveries of machinery and equipment — A	27														12																	12
D	8														2	6	4														12
R	10																	1.5	1.5	1.5	1.5	1.5	1.5	1.5	1.5						12.0
I	2																	0.2	0.2	0.1	0.1	0.1	0.1	0.1	0.1						1.2
LO																10	4	0													
Agreement on economic and technical co-operation — A	31																														6
D																															6
R	10																			0.1	0.6	0.6	0.6	0.6	0.6	0.6	0.6	0.6	0.6	0.6	6.0
I	24																	0.1		0.1	0.1	0.1	0.1	0.1	0.1	0.1	0.1	0.1			0.8
LO																		5	4	3	2	1	0								
TOTALS — A								22							12	6	7	1	1	1	1	1	2	1	1	1					40
D	38								1	3	5	2	1	1	3	6	7														38
R									1				1.0	1.0	1.0	1.0	1.0	2.7	2.7	2.7	3.3	3.3	3.3	3.7	3.4	1.6	1.3	1.0	1.0	1.0	36.0
I										0.1		0.1	0.1	0.1	0.1	0.3	0.3	0.5	0.4	0.4	0.4	0.4	0.4	0.3	0.3	0.2	0.3	0.2	0.3	0.1	5.4
LO								22	22	21	18	13	11	10	9	18	18	11	10	9	8	7	7	4	3						2
Soviet Foreign Trade Statistics — D									0.1	2.6	3.8	1.0	0.4	0.4	0.1	0.9	2.0	0.6	0.6	0.7	0.4	0.6	0.9	1.0	0.4	–	...	0.1	0.1	1.0	16.1

SYRIA

The Soviet Union signed a general economic co-operation agreement in 1957 which established the terms for the next few credits and outlined the projects to be undertaken. The first protocol in 1964 extended a credit mainly for the development of oil and gas prospecting, the construction of a fertilizer plant, and the laying of a railway from Al Qamushli through Aleppo to Latakia. Two separate agreements in 1966 offered a credit of 120m roubles for the construction of a dam, an irrigation scheme, and a hydro-electric power station on the Euphrates, but it is assumed that it was a single credit; the $29m credit in 1972 was for a high tension line and irrigation schemes connected with this project.

The 1972 credits of $25m and $30m were two parts of the same agreement on the development of the Syrian oil industry. The first was for the import of Soviet commodities for sale in Syria to generate funds to help meet the expenses of Soviet specialists; the second—on slightly stiffer terms—was for Syrian purchases of materials and equipment.

In 1974 a wide-ranging credit was agreed to cover the oil, power, transport, and chemical industries, and irrigation. The 1975 agreement allotted 15m roubles to irrigation, fisheries research, and training, and also increased the credits for the Euphrates project by 6m roubles. A further 20m roubles was allotted to this under the 1978 credit.

The 1977 credit was for the large-scale Meskene irrigation project. The last credit, in 1981, was for the construction of two new railway lines, some small hydro-electric power stations for rural electrification, agriculture, and technical training. A protocol to this agreement signed in May 1983 mentioned no new credits, and therefore probably drew on this 1981 credit.

All agreements except that for 1981 were contained in the Soviet Treaty series, although the figure of 60m roubles ($82m) for the 1977 agreement was not, but did appear in the official Soviet publication *Vedomosti Verkhovnogo Soveta* No. 36 of 6 September 1978. Details of the 1981 agreement were given by TASS on 14 May 1981.

Agreement		T	55	56	57	58	59	60	61	62	63	64	65	66	67	68	69	70	71	72	73	74	75	76	77	78	79	80	81	82	83	55-83
Protocol to Agreement on econ'c and tech'l co-operation of 28th Oct 1957	A	41										88																				88
	D											88																				88
	R	5 + 7												2	3	15	18	25	20	5												88
	I	2½												0.1	0.3	0.6	0.8	1.2	1.5	1.5	1.5	1.5	1.5	1.5	1.0	1.0	1.0	1.0	1.0		17
	LO											88	88	86	83	68	50	25	5	0												
Agree't on econ'ic and tech'l co-op'n in construction of 1st stage of HEP & dam on Euphrates	A	34												133																		133
	D														2	3	5	8	20	20	20	20	15	10	8	2						133
	R	12																			11	11	11	11	11	11	11	11	11	11	11	121
	I	2½																			1.8	2.0	2.0	2.0	2.0	2.0	2.0	2.0	2.0	2.0	2.0	24.0
	LO													133	133	131	128	123	115	95	75	55	35	20	10	2	0					0
Agreement on extension of econ'c and tech'l co-operation 1971-75 (i)	A	34																		25												25
	D																				2	5	5	5	5	3						25
	R	12																								2	2	2	2	2	2	12
	I	2½																					0.2	0.2	0.3	0.4	0.4	0.4	0.4	0.3	0.2	3.0
	LO																			25	23	18	13	8	3	0						0
Agreement on extension of econ'c and tech'l co-operation 1971-75 (ii)	A	27																		30												30
	D																				1	4	15	8	2							30
	R	8																							3	3	3	3	3	3	3	21
	I	2½																				0.1	0.2	0.3	0.4	0.4	0.4	0.4	0.4	0.4	0.4	3.4
	LO																				30	29	25	10	2	0						0
Agreement on economic and technical co-operation	A	34																		29												29
	D																				2	8	15	4								29
	R	12																						2.5	2.5	2.6	2.6	2.6	2.6	2.6	2.6	20.6
	I	2½																				0.3	0.4	0.4	0.5	0.5	0.5	0.5	0.5	0.5	0.5	4.6
	LO																			29	27	19										
Long term Agree't on further dev't of economic and technical co-operation	A	34																				140										140
	D																						2	10	25	25	25	25	20	8		140
	R	12																									4	6	8	10	12	40
	I	2½																								2	2	2	2	2		10
	LO																					140	140	138	128	103	78	53	28	8		

		T	55	56	57	58	59	60	61	62	63	64	65	66	67	68	69	70	71	72	73	74	75	76	77	78	79	80	81	82	83	55-83
Agreement on economic and technical co-operation (i)	A	34																					21									21
	D																							4	5	4	4	4	1	2	2	21
	R	12																										0.3	0.3	0.3	0.3	8
	I	2½																									0.3	0.3	0.3	0.3	0.3	1.5
	LO																							21	17	12	8	4	0			
Agreement on economic and technical co-operation (ii)	A	34																					8									8
	D																							3	3	2						8
	R	12																									0.6	0.6	0.6	0.6	0.6	3.0
	I	2½																							0.1		0.2	0.1	0.1	0.1	0.1	0.7
	LO																							8	5	2	0					
Agreement on economic and technical co-operation	A	34																							82							82
	D																								2	2	5	10	20	20	20	77
	R	12																													5	5
	I	2½																									0.1	0.3	0.6	1.0	2.0	4.0
	LO																								82	82	80	75	65	45	25	5
Protocol on economic and technical co-operation	A	27																								27						27
	D																										6	8	8	5		27
	R	8																													3	3
	I	2½																										0.1	0.2	0.3	0.3	0.9
	LO																										27	21	13	5	0	
Railway project and agricultural training centre	*A	31																											56			56
	D	10																												2	15	17
	R	2½																														
	I	2½																														
	LO																													56	54	39

	T	55	56	57	58	59	60	61	62	63	64	65	66	67	68	69	70	71	72	73	74	75	76	77	78	79	80	81	82	83	55-83
TOTALS A											88		133						84		140	29		82	27		47	56			639
D												2	3	17	21	30	28	25	22	31	44	41	40	48	38	40	47	48	35	35	595
R																				11.0	11.0	23.0	25.5	28.5	31.6	37.2	39.2	42.2	31.2	41.2	321.6
I													0.1	0.3	0.7	1.0	1.5	2.1	2.5	3.4	4.0	4.2	4.4	4.3	4.3	6.9	7.1	7.5	6.9	7.9	69.1
LO												88	86	216	199	178	148	120	95	157	126	222	210	170	204	193	153	106	114	79	44
Soviet Foreign Trade Statistics D					2	1	2	9	2	2	1	4	6	21	17	24	22		35	37	36	39	36	37	31	34	33	32	32	31	523.7

TANZANIA

According to Goldman and Müller there was talk of a 38m rouble credit from the Soviet Union to Tanzania in 1964, which would have had an equivalent value of $42m, but there is no evidence of the signature, and some may have been for military equipment. The first economic co-operation agreement in the Soviet Treaty series was for an 18m rouble credit in May 1966 on the standard Soviet terms. This agreement proposed projects for fish drying, four refrigeration units, veterinary centres, geological and hydrological surveys, and an incubator, and trade credits for the purchase of construction and geological equipment and to cover some of the local costs. There is no evidence of any of these projects being realized, though some Soviet experts may have gone to Tanzania under this agreement.

A 1977 protocol to the 1966 agreement offered a new credit of 14m roubles for agricultural machinery, repair shops, housing, and technical training, apparently in the context of the establishment of two state farms.

A new agreement in 1983 offered a new credit, but not on 'aid' terms; it also arranged for the rescheduling of Tanzanian debts.

All agreements in the tables were in the Soviet Treaty series.

		T	55	56	57	58	59	60	61	62	63	64	65	66	67	68	69	70	71	72	73	74	75	76	77	78	79	80	81	82	83	55–83
Agreement on economic and technical co-operation and Protocol	A	34												23	1	2	1	1	1	1	1	1										23
	D																															8
	R	12																		0.6	0.6	0.6	0.6	0.7	0.7	0.7	0.7	0.7	0.7	0.7	0.7	8.0
	I	24																0.1		0.2	0.1	0.1	0.1	0.1	0.1	0.1	0.1	0.1	0.1	0.1	0.1	1.4
	LO	24													23	22	20	19	18	17	16	15	15	15	15	15	15	15	15	15	15	15
Protocol to Agreement on econ'c and tech'l co-operation of 26th May 1966	A	34																							19	1	2	2	3	3	3	19
	D	12																														14
	R	12																0.1										0.1		0.1	0.1	0.3
	I	24																	18							19	18	16	14	11	8	5
	LO	24												23																			
T O T A L S	A													23	1	2	1	1	1	1	1	1			19	1	2	2	3	3	3	42
	D																															22
	R																			0.6	0.6	0.6	0.6	0.7	0.7	0.7	0.7	0.7	0.7	0.7	0.7	8.0
	I																	0.1		0.2	0.1	0.1	0.1	0.1	0.1	0.1	0.1	0.2	0.1	0.2	0.2	1.7
	LO													23	23	22	20	19	18	17	16	15	15	15	15	34	33	31	29	26	23	20
Soviet Foreign Trade Statistics	D																	0.1	0.2	0.6												0.9

TUNISIA

The Soviet Union and Tunisia signed their first trade and payments agreement in January 1961. In the following year the first economic and technical co-operation agreement was signed with the usual twelve-year credit but with an interest rate of 3%, slightly higher than the usual Soviet practice at that time of $2\frac{1}{2}$%. This credit was aimed mainly at the construction of a dam, a hydro-electric power station and irrigation on the Kasseb river, hydrological work in the Ishkel region, and the equipment of a technical school.

In 1976 it was stated in a new agreement that $14\frac{1}{2}$m roubles of the 1961 agreement remained unspent; this sum was now added to a new credit of 27m roubles, still at 3% but with a longer life of fifteen years. The new agreement continued the Kasseb project and the hydrological work, proposed some more dams, and provided the equipment for the enlargement of the technical school. A trade credit was incorporated in this agreement of 15m roubles ($20m) for the purchase of Soviet equipment, but being repayable in eight years it only just remained on 'aid' terms.

Both agreements were published in the Soviet Treaty series.

Note G: This residual was transferred to the 1976 (i) agreement.

	T	55	56	57	58	59	60	61	62	63	64	65	66	67	68	69	70	71	72	73	74	75	76	77	78	79	80	81	82	83	55–83
Agreement on economic and technical co-operation (i) — A	32							28															-166								12
D																															12
R	12								2	3	3	2	2																		12
I	3								0.1	0.1	0.1	0.2	0.2	0.2	0.2	0.2	0.1	0.1	0.1	0.1	0.1	0.1	0.1								2.0
LO									28	26	23	20	18	16	16	16	16	16	16	16	16	16	16								
Agreement on economic and technical co-operation (ii) — A	36																						56	6	10	10	10	10	10		56
D																															56
R	15																									2	2	3	4	4	13
I	3																							0.2	0.3	0.5	1.0	1.0	1.0	1.0	5.0
LO																								56	50	40	30	20	10	0	
Agreement on economic and technical co-operation — A	25																						20								20
D																															20
R	8																							4	4	4	4	2	3	3	11
I	3																							0.1	0.2	0.4	0.4	0.3	0.3	0.3	2.0
LO																								20	16	12	8	4			
T O T A L S — A								28															60								88
D																															88
R									2	3	3	2	2	1	1	1	1	1	1	1	1	1	1	4	4	1	4	5	7	7	36
I									0.1	0.1	0.1	0.2	0.2	0.2	0.2	0.2	0.1	0.1	0.1	0.1	0.1	0.1	0.1	0.3	0.5	0.9	1.4	1.3	1.3	1.3	9.0
LO									28	26	23	20	18	16	16	16	16	16	16	16	16	16	16	76	66	52	38	24	10	0	
Soviet Foreign Trade Statistics — D										0.7		2.2	2.9	1.0	0.7	0.2											9.8	3.3	1.7	1.4	23.9

TURKEY

Turkey has been a major recipient of Soviet economic assistance. Apart from Mongolia she was the only less developed country to receive Soviet assistance before the Second World War; this was a credit in 1934 of $8m to build textile mills, but this is excluded from the table. A trade agreement signed in 1937 was revived by a protocol of March 1960, thus restoring the two countries' economic relations to a formal footing.

The first post-war Soviet assistance to Turkey was offered in 1962 for the construction of a glass factory at Çayirova, south of Istanbul. The interest rate was the Soviet standard $2\frac{1}{2}\%$, but the repayment period was shorter than usual, six and a half years, which brought the concessionality down to the 25% limit of 'aid' terms.

In December 1963 the first major framework agreement on economic co-operation between the two countries was signed. This listed the projects to be undertaken, and gave an outline of the terms although these could be varied when the amount of the credit was agreed under the contracts for specific projects. A similar type of agreement was signed in 1977 with a potential credit given as $1000m or more.

By the time of the signature of the first framework agreement in 1963 preliminary studies were already under way for the construction of the 'Izdemir' integrated iron and steel works at Iskenderun, on the southern Mediterranean coast. Construction started in earnest in 1967, and the first stage was opened in 1975 with a capacity of 1.1m tonnes of steel. Later agreements in 1972 and 1976 were for doubling the capacity.

A second major Soviet-assisted project is the Seydisehir aluminium plant in Konya province. The first stage was constructed between 1968 and 1971, and included a hydro-electric power station at Oymapinar and the supply high-tension line. A $200m credit in 1982 for doubling the capacity of the power station and aluminium plant was on terms of 5% interest repayable in ten years, which brings the concessionality below the 'aid' limit.

The third large Soviet project is the crude oil and part of the downstream capacity of the Aliağa oil refinery near İzmir. Although the majority of the capital and equipment came from other countries, the Soviet input of $25m in 1963 was already considerable; the 1977 framework agreement adumbrated the doubling of the capacity, but the contracts had not been signed by the end of 1983.

Other Soviet-assisted projects were two chemical plants at Bandirma,

		T	55	56	57	58	59	60	61	62	63	64	65	66	67	68	69	70	71	72	73	74	75	76	77	78	79	80	81	82	83	55-83
Cayirova glass factory	*A	25								4																						4
	D									4																						4
	R	6½														0.6	0.6	0.6	0.6	0.6	0.6	0.4										4.0
	I	2½														0.1	0.1	0.1	0.1													0.4
	LO															0				0												
Aliaga Oil Refinery Izmir	*A	37									25																					25
	D															5	8	9	3													25
	R	15																		1.6	1.6	1.6	1.6	1.6	1.6	1.6	1.6	1.6	1.6	1.6	1.6	19.2
	I	2½														0.1	0.2	0.3	0.3	0.4	0.4	0.4	0.4	0.3	0.4	0.3	0.3	0.3	0.3	0.3	0.3	5.0
	LO											25	25	25	25	20	12	3														
Artvin Fibre Board Factory	*A	37									3																					3
	D																																3
	R	15																		0.3	0.3	0.3	0.3	0.3	0.3	0.3	0.3	0.3				2.7
	I	2½																		0.1	0.1	0.1	0.1	0.1	0.1							0.6
	LO											3	3	3	3	3	2	1														
Bandirma Sulphuric Acid Plant	*A	37									3																					3
	D																																3
	R	15																			0.2	0.2	0.2	0.2	0.2	0.2	0.2	0.2	0.2	0.2	0.2	2.2
	I	2½																		0.1	0.1	0.1	0.1	0.1	0.1							0.6
	LO											3	3	3	3	3	3	2	1													
'Isdemir' Iron and Steel Works, Iskenderun	*A	37									100					57	126															283
	D															5	10	70	100	70	20	8										283
	R	15																														192
	I	2½															1.0	1.5	2.0	3.8	3.8	3.8	3.8	3.8	3.8	3.8	3.8	3.8	3.8	3.8	3.8	50.1
	LO															152	268	198	98	28	8											
Seydisehir Aluminium Plant	*A	37									78																					78
	D															25	40	13															78
	R	15																	5.2	5.2	5.2	5.2	5.2	5.2	5.2	5.2	5.2	5.2	5.2	5.2	5.2	67.6
	I	2½																	1.1	1.1	1.1	1.1	1.1	1.1	1.1	1.0	1.0	1.0	1.0	1.0	1.0	13.7
	LO										78	78	78	78	78	53	13															

of which the first was a sulphuric acid plant completed in 1971 with a credit on aid terms, but the second, a hydrogen peroxide plant, had a credit which was not; and a fibre board plant at Artvin. Agreement was also reached for the construction of a thermal power station at Orhaneli, and another proposed at Keles in Bursa province, but neither were under construction by the end of 1983.

A Soviet-assisted project of a different order is the development of a dam, reservoir, and hydro-electric project on the river Arpaçay (Akhuryan) where it forms the frontier between Turkey and Soviet Armenia. Discussion of the project had already been mentioned in the early 1960s, but the first official agreement was apparently not signed until 1973. This agreement gave the cost of the work to be undertaken as 16.6m roubles, with each country paying half; the Soviet Union agreed, however, to pay half of the Turkish share as a gift. In 1980 the next stage was agreed; the cost was given as 140m roubles, with the Turkish half being looked after by an interest-free credit repayable in twelve years. By the end of 1983 the dam and most of the reservoir had been completed.

The Çayirova agreement was given with full details by Müller, who also gave details of the 1963 framework agreement. All other agreements except those for the Arpaçay project were reported by the Turkish Consortium to the OECD. Goldman spoke of an Arpaçay agreement for a $15m credit in 1964, but this was not confirmed and no work seems to have been undertaken before the 1973 agreement, which was published in the Soviet Treaty series; the 1981 agreement was published in the press and on the radio—for example, Radio Anatolia of 30 March 1981. The 1977 framework agreement mentioned in the text was published in the Soviet Treaty series and in the Soviet official *Vedomosti Verkhovnogo Soveta* of 17 May 1978.

		T	55	56	57	58	59	60	61	62	63	64	65	66	67	68	69	70	71	72	73	74	75	76	77	78	79	80	81	82	83	55–83
Oymapinar Hydroelectric Power Station for Seydisehir	*A	34														29																29.0
	D																		8	12	9											29.0
	R	12																				2.4	2.4	2.4	2.4	2.4	2.4	2.4	2.4	2.4	2.4	24.0
	I	2½																				0.4	0.4	0.4	0.4	0.4	0.4	0.4	0.4	0.4	0.4	4.0
	LO																															
'Isdemir' Iron and Steel Works, Iskenderun (cont'd)	*A	34																		158				113								271
	D																					5	6	8	25	50	75	50	30	20	2	271
	R	12																									12	18	22	22	22	96
	I	2½																						1.0	1.5	2.0	3.0	3.7	3.7	3.7	3.7	22.3
	LO																				158	158	153	147	252	227	177	102	52	22	2	0
Agreement on constructing a dam and reservoir on River Arpacay at frontier	*A	100																			5											5
	D																					5										5
	R	–																				1	2	2								
	I	–																														
	LO																					5	4	2	0							
Orhaneli Thermal Power Station	*A	31																									53					53
	D																															
	R	10																														
	I	2½																														
	LO																															
Arpacay Dam and Hydroelectric Project	*A	45																										53	53	53	53	53
	D																												88			88
	R	12																												10	30	40
	I	–																														
	LO																															48

	T	55	56	57	58	59	60	61	62	63	64	65	66	67	68	69	70	71	72	73	74	75	76	77	78	79	80	81	82	83	55-83
TOTALS A									4	209				4	86	126	96	113	158	5	14	8	113			53		88			842
D															35	58			82	29			10	25	50	75	50	30	30	32	741
R															0.6	0.6	0.6	5.8	14.9	14.9	17.1	28.6	28.6	28.6	28.6	40.6	46.6	50.6	50.5	50.5	407.7
I															0.2	1.2	1.9	3.4	5.6	5.3	6.0	5.7	6.8	7.2	7.7	8.5	9.4	9.2	9.4	9.2	96.7
LO											213	213	213	213	209	260	328	232	119	195	171	157	149	252	227	177	155	105	163	133	101
Soviet Foreign Trade Statistics D					0.2	1.2	3.7	1.4	0.2	0.1			0.1		3.6	24.4	37.0		114	96.7	30.5	11.2	12.7	34.5	56.6	85.2	95.0	65.6	60.4	31.4	765.7

UGANDA

The first Soviet economic co-operation agreement with Uganda was signed in 1964. It offered a credit of 14m roubles, or £5.6m sterling, for a cotton combine, a milk factory, refrigeration units, equipment for a veterinary centre, and some tractors and bulldozers, and to provide a technical report on the feasibility of a fish cannery. Apart from the cotton spinning plant, which was operating in 1977, there have been few reports of the implementation of these projects. A protocol to this agreement in 1972 rescheduled Ugandan debts—although the amounts are marginal and have been ignored in the table; and a further protocol was agreed for a new credit in 1978—the amount was not given, but has been assumed to have been $2m.

In April 1983 the Soviet ambassador to Kampala announced a new $11m credit, and in August the signature of a new economic co-operation agreement was announced; these two reports are assumed to have referred to the same agreement, and the terms to be the same as for the 1978 agreement.

The first two agreements were published in the Soviet Treaty series, although the amount was not given for the second. The Soviet ambassador's mention of an $11m credit was announced on Kampala radio on 4 March, and the signature of the agreement on Moscow radio on 29 August 1983.

		T	55	56	57	58	59	60	61	62	63	64	65	66	67	68	69	70	71	72	73	74	75	76	77	78	79	80	81	82	83	55-83
Agreement on economic and technical co-operation	A	34										16																				16
	D	12																														12
	R	12													1	1	1	1	4	1	1	1	1								12
	I	2½														0.1		0.1	0.2	0.3	0.3	0.2	0.2	0.2	0.2	0.2	0.2	0.2	0.2	0.2	0.2	3.0
	LO												16	16	16	15	14	13	12	8	7	6	5	4	4	4	4	4	4	4	4	4
Protocol to Agreement on econ'c and tech'l co-op'n in sphere of geolog'l prospecting work	A	27																								2						2
	D																										0.5					0.5
	R	10																										...	...	...	...	...
	I	3½																										...	...	...	...	...
	LO	3½																									2.0	1.5	1.5	1.5	1.5	1.5
Agreement on economic and technical co-operation	*A	27																													11	11
	D																															
	R	10																														
	I	3½																														
	LO	3½																													11	11
TOTALS	A											16														2					11	29
	D																										0.5					0.5
	R															1	1	1	1	4	1	1	1	1								12.5
	I															0.1		0.1	0.2	0.3	0.3	0.2	0.2	0.2	0.2	0.2	0.2	0.2	0.2	0.2	0.2	3.0
	LO												16	16	16	15	14	13	12	8	7	6	5	4	4	4	6.0	5.5	5.5	5.5	5.5	16.5
Soviet Foreign Trade Statistics	D														0.2	0.3	...	0.4		3.5	...	0.3	0.6	0.6	0.1							6.0

VIETNAM

The first Soviet agreement with North Vietnam on economic co-operation was signed in 1960, and set out the general terms for future collaboration in the 'construction and extension of a series of industrial undertakings and projects and the supply of equipment and materials'. A 1962 protocol to this agreement set aside 10m roubles to be used in 1966–68 for tractors, fuel, tropical fertilizers, and further technical co-operation.

Three agreements in July, September, and December 1965 gave grants of 'approximately' 17.5m, 2.8m, and 38.5m roubles respectively for the purchase of the goods listed in the (unpublished) annex. In October two new interest-free loans of 127m and 25m roubles were extended for the purchase of Soviet goods at world prices; the first repayable in twenty years and the second in fifteen. A protocol to this agreement six months later altered the ratio to 125m and 27m roubles respectively, and these are the figures in the table; it stated that the credits would be used for a thermal-electric power station at Yong Bi, for coalmining, for a 100mm pipeline, and for a helicopter.

In 1972 a new credit was agreed offering equipment and 'brigades' for bridge-building, road-making, aerodromes, quarrying, irrigation, drilling, oil reservoirs, communications, and several other projects of a lesser nature. It also rescheduled some of Vietnam's debts, although for various reasons, this is ignored in the table. In 1973 the last agreement to give the amount of the credit was published; it catered for the despatch of eight thousand Vietnamese between the ages of sixteen and twenty-five to study in the USSR between 1973 and 1976.

Two other agreements were reached with Vietnam in 1978 and 1979 covering a wide range of economic co-operation, but no amounts were given. From 1974 onwards, therefore, estimates of Soviet economic assistance to Vietnam have perforce been based on the Soviet tables of deliveries under economic and technical co-operation agreements in their annual trade statistics. It must be assumed that all these deliveries were on aid terms, and did not include military equipment; a proportion has been added to include technical assistance which *a priori* is not included in deliveries.

The 1960 agreement was not published in the Soviet Treaty series, but was referred to in some detail by the 1962 protocol to that agreement which was. All other agreements mentioned above were listed in the Soviet Treaty series. Goldman refers to a '$100m credit' being

Agreement		T	55	56	57	58	59	60	61	62	63	64	65	66	67	68	69	70	71	72	73	74	75	76	77	78	79	80	81	82	83	55–83
Agreement and Protocol on extension of econ'c and tech'l co-operation	*A	41						100	40	40																						100
	D																															
	R	15						10	40	40	6.0	6.0	6.0	6.0	6.0	6.0	6.7	6.7	6.7	6.7	6.7	6.7	6.7	6.7	6.7	0.7	0.6	0.6	0.6	0.6	0.6	100.0
	I	2						0.1	0.2	0.5	1.0	1.0	1.0	1.1	1.2	1.2	1.2	1.2	1.1	1.1	1.1	1.1	1.1	1.1	1.1	1.1	0.1	0.1	0.1	0.1	0.1	18.0
	LO							0	90	50	10	10	10	10	7	4	2	0														
Agreement on extension of supplementary free economic assistance	A	100											19																			19
	D												12	7																		19
	R	–																														–
	I	–																														–
	LO												7	0																		–
Pro'col to Agree't on ext'n of free supplementary econ'c assistance of 10th July 1965	A	100											3																			3
	D												2	1																		3
	R	–																														–
	I	–																														–
	LO												1	0																		–
Agreement on-extension of supplementary free economic assistance	A	100												43																		43
	D													30	13																	43
	R	–																														–
	I	–																														–
	LO													13	0																	–
Agreement and Protocol on economic and technical assistance (i)	A	59															139															139
	D																	69	70													139
	R	20																		7	7	7	7	7	7	7	7	7	7	7	7	84
	I	–																														–
	LO																139	70	0													–
Agreement and Protocol on economic and technical assistance (ii)	A	51																30														30
	D																		15	15												30
	R	15																		2	2	2	2	2	2	2	2	2	2	2	2	24
	I	–																														–
	LO																	30	15	0												–

offered in 1955, and quotes the Russians as claiming to have offered credits (including a gift of $105m) totalling $350m by 1961; but there is no evidence of the purpose, which could have been at least partially military, or the terms, which might not have been all 'aid'. The evidence of the Soviet Treaty series has therefore been taken.

	T	55	56	57	58	59	60	61	62	63	64	65	66	67	68	69	70	71	72	73	74	75	76	77	78	79	80	81	82	83	55–83
Agreement on extension of economic and technical assistance — A	67																		11												11
D																				11											11
R	5 +15																								0.7	0.7	0.7	0.7	0.7	0.7	4.2
I	–																														–
LO	–																														
Agreement on extension of assistance in workers' training — A	100																			47											•47
D																				2	15	15	15								47
R	–																														
I	–																				0			0							
LO																					45	30	15	0							
Assumed annual agreements from Soviet Foreign Trade Statistics — *A	100						100					65				169			11		60	68	87	111	153	254	257	212	284	220	1706
D							10	40	40			14	41	16	2	2	84	85		13	75	83	102	111	153	254	257	212	284	220	1706
R	–																														
I	–																														
LO	–																														
TOTALS — A							100					65				169			11		60	68	87	111	153	254	257	212	284	220	2098
D							10	40	40			14	41	16	2	2	84	85		13	75	83	102	111	153	254	257	212	284	220	2098
R										6.0	6.0	6.0	6.0	6.0	6.0	6.7	6.7	6.7	15.7	15.7	15.7	15.7	15.7	15.7	10.4	10.3	10.3	10.3	10.3	10.3	212.2
I							0.1	0.2	0.5	1.0	1.0	1.0	1.1	1.2	1.2	1.2	1.2	1.1	1.1	1.1	1.1	1.1	1.1	1.1	0.1	0.1	0.1	0.1	0.1	0.1	18.0
LO							90	90	50		10	10	61	20	4	2	169	85		11	45	30	15	0							
Soviet Foreign Trade Statistics — D				..	..	..	3	12	22	24	36	32	34	43	30	34	28		9	13	41	45	58	75	102	176	178	141	189	147	1472

YEMEN ARAB REPUBLIC

The first Soviet assistance to North Yemen was offered in 1956; it considered a wide range of projects, and was probably mainly taken up with feasibility studies and other technical assistance. The small 1962 credit was also for feasibility studies, and led to the main Soviet credit in 1964 under which the major Soviet projects in North Yemen were built: the Hodeida–Taiz road, the Bajil cement plants, and the Hodeida port development. In addition the credit allowed for a fish processing factory and geological prospecting. The 1971 credit was a supplement to the 1964 agreement.

Soviet economic co-operation with North Yemen continued with a 7m rouble ($10m) credit in 1981 for various hydrological schemes, and a protocol to this agreement in 1982 offering 17m roubles ($23m) for the reconstruction of the Hodeida–Taiz road; but at 5% interest with ten years to repay this did not qualify as aid, and in any case was apparently not taken up.

The 1956 agreement was reported in Goldman (who gave the amount as $20m) and Müller. Müller gave the 1961 agreement as $2.5m; the confirmation of Müller's $15m in 1956, and the $0.5m (suggesting an earlier confusion between old and new roubles) came orally from the Soviet economic co-operation experts in Sana'a. The 1964 agreement was published in the Soviet Treaty series, and the December 1971 credit of $8m was reported in INA on 2 March 1972. The two non-'aid' agreements mentioned in the paragraph above were in the Soviet Treaty series.

Category		T	55	56	57	58	59	60	61	62	63	64	65	66	67	68	69	70	71	72	73	74	75	76	77	78	79	80	81	82	83	55–83
Cement, electrical power, ports, and agricultural projects	*A	34		15																												15
	D					1	2	2		1	1	1	1	2	2	2																15
	R	12							0.5	0.5	0.5	0.5	1.0	1.0	1.0	1.0	1.0	1.0	1.0	1.0	1.0	1.0	1.0	1.0	1.0							15.0
	I	2½								0.2	0.2	0.1	0.1	0.1	0.2	0.2	0.2	0.2	0.2	0.2	0.2				0.5	0.5						2.4
	LO				15	15	14	12	10	9	8	7	6	5	3	1	0															
Ports, roads, and irrigation	*A																															0.5
	D									0.5																						0.5
	R									0.2	0.2	0.1																				0.5
	I											0.1																				0.1
	LO								0.5	0.5	0.3	0.1																				
Agreement on economic and technical co-operation	A	51										72																				72
	D											2	15	15	10	10	10	10														72
	R	15																														67
	I	–																														–
	LO											72	70	55	40	30	20	10	0													–
Completion of projects and start of new projects	*A	34																									1	3	4			8
	D																										1	3	4			8
	R	12																												0.7	0.7	1.4
	I	2½																												0.2	0.1	0.3
	LO																		8	8	8	8	8	8	8	8	8	7	4	0		
TOTALS	A			15.0						0.5		72.0															1.0	3.0	4.0			95.5
	D					1.0	2.0	2.0	1.0	1.2	1.2	3.1	16.0	17.0	12.0	11.0	11.0	10.0														95.5
	R								0.5	0.7	0.7	0.6	1.0	1.1	1.0	1.1	1.1	3.1	6.0	6.1	6.0	6.0	6.0	6.0	5.5	5.5	5.0	5.0	5.0	5.7	5.7	83.9
	I									0.2	0.2	0.2	0.2	0.2	0.2	0.2	0.2	0.3	0.2	0.2	0.2	0.2	0.2	0.2	0.2	0.2				0.2	0.1	2.8
	LO				15.0	15.0	14.0	12.0	10.0	9.5	8.3	7.1	76.0	60.0	43.0	31.0	20.0	11.0	8.0	8.0	8.0	8.0	8.0	8.0	8.0	8.0	8.0	7.0	4.0	0.0		
Soviet Foreign Trade Statistics	D					0.5	2.0	2.1	0.5	0.1	0.1	0.3	1.5	5.4	6.1	2.1	3.7	4.4		0.9	0.7	0.6	1.5	1.8	0.8	0.5	8.7	8.9	8.6	3.7	2.8	89.3

YEMEN PEOPLE'S DEMOCRATIC REPUBLIC

With only one percent of its land cultivable it was not surprising that the first Soviet economic co-operation in 1969 was concerned with irrigation and other agricultural objectives. In 1972 a new credit, on more generous terms than the Soviet standard at the time, was extended for a thermal power station in Aden, equipment for a hospital, and the development of Aden airport. The first 1975 credit, in June, was for oil prospecting and the second, in November, was to continue irrigation work and aerial surveys.

The 1976 agreement consolidated the 1969, 1972, and the two 1975 agreements, as well as two unpublished agreements of 1971 and 1974, into one single agreement and added a further 18m roubles. The purpose of the increase was the purchase of Soviet goods to be sold in South Yemen to help cover local Soviet costs; each of the previous agreements had also had a proportion of their credits allocated to this purpose, and the practice continued with the later agreements. A 1977 protocol to this agreement was to extend the surveys for water and soil resources and for oil exploration in the Hadramut valley.

The 1978 credit of 63m roubles was destined for a series of projects, including the Aden power station, the formation of a construction company, further work on irrigation, and a cement factory. The 1979 agreement added 18m roubles to the June 1975 agreement and 45m roubles to the (unpublished) agreement of 31 January 1979. The former was to continue oil exploration, the latter was to develop communications—radio, television, telephones, and telex.

The 1972 agreement had spoken of work on a power station near Aden at Al Hiswah; the first stage was to be of 50MW capacity with the possibility of expansion by a further 50MW. The 1978 agreement also allocated some of its credit to this project, and the 1980 and 1982 credits of 110m and 80m roubles respectively were completely given over to it.

The main projects assisted by the Russians in South Yemen have been the Aden power station, irrigation, Aden airport, cement, oil prospecting, and the communications already mentioned, and they were also involved in the development of the port of Aden, the construction of a printing works and fish cannery, and in technical training centres.

All the agreements were published in the Soviet Treaty series except two in 1971 and 1974; these were referred to in later agreements, but nothing else is known about them.

		T	55	56	57	58	59	60	61	62	63	64	65	66	67	68	69	70	71	72	73	74	75	76	77	78	79	80	81	82	83	55–83
Agreement on economic and technical co-operation	A	38															8			1	1	1	1	3								8
	D																															
	R	2 +12																	0.1						0.1	0.7	0.7	0.7	0.7	0.7	0.7	4.2
	I	24																	0.1					0.1	0.1	0.1	0.1	0.1	0.1	0.1	0.1	1.0
	LO	24																8	8	7	6	5	4	3	0							
Agreement on economic and technical co-operation	A	38																		17				4								17
	D																															
	R	2 +12																					5			1.4	1.4	1.4	1.4	1.4	1.4	8.4
	I	24																				0.1	0.1	0.1	0.2	0.2	0.2	0.2	0.2	0.2	0.2	1.6
	LO	24																			17	13	9	4	0							
Agreement on co-operation in carrying out oil prospecting work	A	56																					12	3	3	3	3	0				12
	D																															
	R	2 +15																											0.8	0.8	0.8	2.4
	I	–																														–
	LO	–																						12	12	9	6	3	0				
Protocol on questions of economic and technical co-operation	A	38																					12	4	4	4	4	1	1	1	1	12
	D																															
	R	2 +12																						4	4	4	1	1	1	1	1	4
	I	24																					0.1	0.1	0.1	0.1	0.2	0.3	0.3	0.3	0.3	1.0
	LO	24																						12	8	4	0					
Protocol to Agreements of 1969, 1971, 1972, and 1974, and to Protocol of 1975	A	38																						24	8	8	8	4	2	2	2	24
	D																							24								
	R	2 +12																							–	8	8	4	2	2	2	6
	I	24																						0.1	0.1	0.2	0.3	0.3	0.3	0.3	0.3	1.8
	LO	24																						24	24	16	8	0				
Protocol on questions of economic and technical co-operation	A	38																							10	10	4	4	2				10
	D																															
	R	2 +12																												0.8	0.8	0.8	1.6
	I	24																										0.1	0.1	0.1	0.2	0.1	0.6
	LO	24																							10	10	6	2	2				

	T	55	56	57	58	59	60	61	62	63	64	65	66	67	68	69	70	71	72	73	74	75	76	77	78	79	80	81	82	83	55-83
Protocol on economic and technical co-operation A	38																								92						92
D																										12	20	20	20	20	92
R	2 +12																														
I	2½																									0.2	0.4	0.6	0.8	1.0	3.0
LO																										92	80	60	40	20	0
Protocol on economic and technical co-operation A	38																									96					96
D																											16	20	20	20	76
R	2 +12																														
I	2½																										0.2	0.4	0.6	0.8	2.0
LO																											96	80	60	40	20
Agreement on co-operation in construction of a thermal power station A	32																										169				169
D																												2	2	10	14
R	2 +10																														
I	3																											0.1	0.1	0.3	0.5
LO																											169	169	167	165	155
Protocol on further extension of economic and technical co-operation A	32																										55				55
D																												10	10	10	30
R	2 +10																														
I	3																											0.3	0.5	0.7	1.5
LO																											55	55	45	35	25
Proto'l to Agree't on economic and technical co-operation of 23rd Sept 1981 A	32																												61		61
D																														10	10
R	2 +10																														
I	3																													0.2	0.2
LO																													61	61	51

	T	55	56	57	58	59	60	61	62	63	64	65	66	67	68	69	70	71	72	73	74	75	76	77	78	79	80	81	82	83	55-83
TOTALS — A																8			17			24	24	10	92	96	224		61		556
TOTALS — D																		1	1	5	5	6	14	15	19	27	38	52	52	70	305
TOTALS — R																									2.1	2.1	3.1	5.9	6.7	6.7	26.6
TOTALS — I																		0.1			0.1	0.2	0.3	0.4	0.6	1.1	1.4	2.2	2.9	3.9	13.2
TOTALS — LO																	8	8	7	23	18	13	31	41	36	109	178	364	312	321	251
Soviet Foreign Trade Statistics — D																			1.4	2.0	1.6	3.3	11.5	25.0	17.8	31.4	33.0	38.0	43.3	76.6	284.9

ZAMBIA

The first Soviet economic co-operation agreement with Zambia, and the only one on 'aid' terms was signed on 26 May 1967. It was in the form of a framework agreement under which contracts were later signed for the delivery of four diesel engines for electric power production, for some medical and engineering equipment for Zambia University, and for the supply of some road-building machinery and equipment. Soviet foreign trade statistics show that goods to a value of $2\frac{1}{2}$m were delivered under this agreement, and it is assumed that the rest was for technical assistance.

In 1972 the number of diesel generators under this credit was raised to six. When the first started operating in 1976 the number promised was again raised to ten, but nothing was said about the financing of the last four.

In April 1983 an agreement was signed for the rescheduling of Zambia's debts; and in July of the same year a new credit was announced for land-clearing equipment, but it was not on 'aid' terms.

		T	55	56	57	58	59	60	61	62	63	64	65	66	67	68	69	70	71	72	73	74	75	76	77	78	79	80	81	82	83	55-83
Agreement on economic and technical co-operation	A	34													6																	6
	D																															
	R	12																				2	2	2	0.5	0.5	0.5	0.5	0.5	0.5	0.5	3.5
	I	24																					0.1		0.1	0.1	0.1	0.1	0.1	0.1	0.1	0.5
	LO															6	6	6	6	6	6	6	4	2	0							
Soviet Foreign Trade Statistics	D																					0.8	0.4	1.2	0.1							2.5

SOURCES

The principle source for the agreements is the Soviet official series of Treaties published by 'Mezhdunarodnyye otnosheniya' in Moscow, backed up occasionally by the 'Vedomosti' of the Supreme Soviet. Some early agreements which were not in these series were in Goldman's *Soviet Foreign Aid* (1967) and Müller's *Handbuch der Entwicklungshilfe UdSSR* (1966). The other agreements came from various press and radio sources.

Some partner data have been shown for reference (Pakistan and Somalia), but this has not generally been acceptable as a main source because of different financial years, and there are other pitfalls such as f.o.b. and c.i.f. prices and various currency exchange rates. The figures given by the Turkish Consortium to the OECD are generally used for that country, however, since they parallel closely the Soviet data and often give more detail.

The background information on all other aspects—disbursements, construction, repayments, interest, and rescheduling—came mainly from the files, and with the active help, of Henryk Bischof of the Friedrich-Ebert-Stiftung in Bonn; he also kindly lent me the book by Müller. Ruth Stock of the OECD in Paris has also made many positive contributions as well as correcting errors. The third main source in these fields has been the personal contacts with individuals at the World Bank and the International Monetary Fund in Washington, and in the sample of twelve countries I was privileged to visit to check the theories, data, and conclusions—Bangladesh, Egypt, Ethiopia, India, Kenya, Nepal, Pakistan, Somalia, Syria, Tanzania, Turkey, and the Yemen Arab Republic. In these countries assistance was not only proffered by government officials of the country concerned but also in most cases by the local representatives of the Soviet organization for economic co-operation—the GKES. A list of published sources and of these individuals follows.

PUBLISHED SOURCES

The Soviet Treaty series: *Sbornik deystvuyushchikh dogovorov* volumes xvii–xxxv, 1954 to 1979 Moscow; *Sbornik mezhdunarodnykh dogovorov* volumes xxxvi–xxxix, 1980 to 1983 Moscow.

Vedomosti Verkhovnogo Soveta: official gazette of the USSR Supreme Soviet for the relevant dates.

Vneshnyaya Torgovlya SSSR: statisticheskiy sbornik: annual.

BBC Summary of World Broadcasts.

F. Müller: *Handbuch der Entwicklungshilfe UdSSR*, published for the government ministries of the German Federal Republic, Bonn 1966.

Marshall I. Goldman: *Soviet Foreign Aid*, Praeger, New York, and London 1967.

Bundesstelle für Aussenhandelsinformation/Nachrichten für Aussenhandel (*BfA/NfA*) 1955–1983, Federal Republic of Germany.

Entwicklungspolitische   Aktivitäten   kommunistischer   Länder,   Forschungsinstitut der Friedrich-Ebert-Stiftung, Bonn 1970–1981.

The following people have personally given useful information which contributed directly to this research:

Forschungs Institut der Friedrich-Ebert-Stiftung, Bonn

H. Bischof

Development Assistance Directorate, OECD, Paris

Miss R. Stock

International Monetary Fund, Washington

M. Williamson
Mohammad Shadman (Pakistan)
Mohammad Zubair Khan (Turkey)
T. Wolf (Economics of Centrally Planned Economies)

World Bank, Washington

S. Lee (Economics and Projection Department)
W. McCleary (ASAPA)
Firoz Vakil (Turkey)
N. C. Hope (Chief, External Debt Division)

Bangladesh

Dr Sayid Abdus Samad, Joint Secretary, MoF
Narul Haq, Assistant Chief, MoF
Aleksandr Tokarev, GKES

Egypt

Shawkat Yanny, Assistant Under Secretary, Ministry of Trade
Mahmoud Hilal, First Deputy Secretary, Ministry of Industry
Ambassador Hassan Kandil, Permanent Secretary, MFA
Dia Tartawy, Managing Director, Helwan Steel Works
Eng. Salah Mohammed Fagal, General Manager, Aswan High Dam Company
G. Lotfy, General Manager, Aluminium Company of Egypt, Nag Hammadi
Zaki Abdo Basuoni, Production Manager, Aluminium Company of Egypt, Nag Hammadi
Fathy Farahat, General Manager, Foreign Department, Central Bank of Egypt
Nikolai Kartouzov, Counsellor, USSR Embassy
Eng. Askold Dralo, GKES

Ethiopia

Michael Payson, World Bank Resident Representative
J. Wallner, Delegate for Economic Aid
Alu Mayo Dany, National Council for Central Planning
Andrej Repin, GKES

India

N. S. Choudhary, Minister Economic, Indian High Commission, London
K. Radha Krishnan, Controller of Accounts and Audit, MoF
Tirlochan Singh, Joint Secretary, Department of Steel
Arwind Varma, Joint Secretary, Department of Petroleum
S. C. Dhingra, Joint Secretary, Department of Heavy Engineering
P. K. Lahiri, Joint Secretary, Department of Coal
V. L. Korneyev, GKES

Kenya

Mr Daugana, Development Aid Department, MoF and Economic Affairs
D. Odede, European and Commonwealth Department, MFA
G. F. Tarasov, GKES
Dmitri Riabovalov, GKES

Nepal

M. Ghimire, Under Secretary, Foreign Aid Division, MoF
Oleg M. Oparin, GKES

Pakistan

Professor Syed Haiden Naqvi, Director, Pakistan Institute of Development
   Economics
M. H. Chaudri, Joint Secretary, Debt Repayment and Re-scheduling, MoF
Osman Sher, Deputy Secretary General, Economic Affairs Division, MoF
M. S. Jillani, Additional Secretary, Ministry of Planning
Mohammad Ahmad Duraishi, General Manager, Public relations, Pakistan
   Steel, Karachi

Somalia

Jurgend Kraft, Delegate for Economic Aid of the European Commission
L. Cohen, Director US Aid
Ms M. Scovell, Economist, US Aid
Abdi Awale Jama, Director of Information and Public Affairs, MFA
Ambassador Ahmed Muhammad Adan, Permanent Secretary, MFA
Mr Abyan, Director, Institute of Development and Management
Dr Mustafa Al Haq, Director of Studies, Insitute of Development and
   Management
Mr Awil, Director of Statistics, MoF

Syria

Thomas C. Sullivan, Delegate for Aid of the European Commission
William N. Witting, First Secretary, Economic Affairs, US Embassy

Tanzania

Mr Mashamgama, First Deputy Under Secretary, Ministry of Finance
A. V. Vodinsky, GKES
V. Kilva, GKES

Turkey

Mehmet Tuncer, Counsellor, Turkish Embassy, London
Ertuğrul Senay, MoF
Sinasi Altiner, General Manager, Iskenderun Iron and Steel Works
Rifat Kont, Managing Director, Seydisehir Aluminium Works
Doğan Toksaltik, Operational Manager, TUPRAS Oil Refinery, İzmir
Orhan Koçanaoğullari, Financial Manager, TUPRAS Oil Refinery, İzmir

Yemen Arab Republic

Scot Robinson, Shell Representative
Christine Abel, World Bank Resident Representative
Victor Burdin, Counsellor, GKES
Vsevolod Fedorov, Counsellor, GKES

MoF = Ministry of Finance; MFA = Ministry of Foreign Affairs; GKES = (USSR) State
Committee for (Foreign) Economic Relations

INDEX OF COUNTRIES